THIS IS YOUR **PASSBOOK**® FOR ...

COLLEGE ADMINISTRATIVE ASSISTANT

NATIONAL LEARNING CORPORATION®
passbooks.com

COPYRIGHT NOTICE

Copyright © 2018 by

NLC®

National Learning Corporation

212 Michael Drive, Syosset, NY 11791
(516) 921-8888 • www.passbooks.com
E-mail: info@passbooks.com

PUBLISHED IN THE UNITED STATES OF AMERICA

PASSBOOK® SERIES

THE *PASSBOOK® SERIES* has been created to prepare applicants and candidates for the ultimate academic battlefield – the examination room.

At some time in our lives, each and every one of us may be required to take an examination – for validation, matriculation, admission, qualification, registration, certification, or licensure.

Based on the assumption that every applicant or candidate has met the basic formal educational standards, has taken the required number of courses, and read the necessary texts, the *PASSBOOK® SERIES* furnishes the one special preparation which may assure passing with confidence, instead of failing with insecurity. Examination questions – together with answers – are furnished as the basic vehicle for study so that the mysteries of the examination and its compounding difficulties may be eliminated or diminished by a sure method.

This book is meant to help you pass your examination provided that you qualify and are serious in your objective.

The entire field is reviewed through the huge store of content information which is succinctly presented through a provocative and challenging approach – the question-and-answer method.

A climate of success is established by furnishing the correct answers at the end of each test.

You soon learn to recognize types of questions, forms of questions, and patterns of questioning. You may even begin to anticipate expected outcomes.

You perceive that many questions are repeated or adapted so that you can gain acute insights, which may enable you to score many sure points.

You learn how to confront new questions, or types of questions, and to attack them confidently and work out the correct answers.

You note objectives and emphases, and recognize pitfalls and dangers, so that you may make positive educational adjustments.

Moreover, you are kept fully informed in relation to new concepts, methods, practices, and directions in the field.

You discover that you arre actually taking the examination all the time: you are preparing for the examination by "taking" an examination, not by reading extraneous and/or supererogatory textbooks.

In short, this PASSBOOK®, used directedly, should be an important factor in helping you to pass your test.

COLLEGE ADMINISTRATIVE ASSISTANT

DUTIES:

Under general direction, is responsible for the operation of a major college activity, performs difficult administrative and/or secretarial work in an office with college-wide responsibilities or in an academic department with unusually complex problems; performs related work.

EXAMPLES OF TYPICAL TASKS:

Develops and maintains efficient office procedures and methods and trains employees in their use. Interprets and applies rules and regulations within a technical area of operation. Acts as responsible head of a major unit of operation. Supervises and coordinates the work of other employees. Confers with staff and/or students concerning a student's academic, personal, placement and health problems. Conducts and assists in conducting interviews. Counsels faculty and administrative staff on pension system, health insurance plans and other welfare and fringe benefit programs. Serves as secretarial assistant to a major administrative officer. Represents the college at meetings and conferences. Prepares periodic and other reports.

TESTS:

The written test will be of the multiple-choice type and may include questions on the operations of the colleges, staff development and supervision, reading comprehension, English usage, interviewing, computations and interpretation of data and office practice.

HOW TO TAKE A TEST

I. YOU MUST PASS AN EXAMINATION

A. WHAT EVERY CANDIDATE SHOULD KNOW

Examination applicants often ask us for help in preparing for the written test. What can I study in advance? What kinds of questions will be asked? How will the test be given? How will the papers be graded?

As an applicant for a civil service examination, you may be wondering about some of these things. Our purpose here is to suggest effective methods of advance study and to describe civil service examinations.

Your chances for success on this examination can be increased if you know how to prepare. Those "pre-examination jitters" can be reduced if you know what to expect. You can even experience an adventure in good citizenship if you know why civil service exams are given.

B. WHY ARE CIVIL SERVICE EXAMINATIONS GIVEN?

Civil service examinations are important to you in two ways. As a citizen, you want public jobs filled by employees who know how to do their work. As a job seeker, you want a fair chance to compete for that job on an equal footing with other candidates. The best-known means of accomplishing this two-fold goal is the competitive examination.

Exams are widely publicized throughout the nation. They may be administered for jobs in federal, state, city, municipal, town or village governments or agencies.

Any citizen may apply, with some limitations, such as the age or residence of applicants. Your experience and education may be reviewed to see whether you meet the requirements for the particular examination. When these requirements exist, they are reasonable and applied consistently to all applicants. Thus, a competitive examination may cause you some uneasiness now, but it is your privilege and safeguard.

C. HOW ARE CIVIL SERVICE EXAMS DEVELOPED?

Examinations are carefully written by trained technicians who are specialists in the field known as "psychological measurement," in consultation with recognized authorities in the field of work that the test will cover. These experts recommend the subject matter areas or skills to be tested; only those knowledges or skills important to your success on the job are included. The most reliable books and source materials available are used as references. Together, the experts and technicians judge the difficulty level of the questions.

Test technicians know how to phrase questions so that the problem is clearly stated. Their ethics do not permit "trick" or "catch" questions. Questions may have been tried out on sample groups, or subjected to statistical analysis, to determine their usefulness.

Written tests are often used in combination with performance tests, ratings of training and experience, and oral interviews. All of these measures combine to form the best-known means of finding the right person for the right job.

II. HOW TO PASS THE WRITTEN TEST

A. NATURE OF THE EXAMINATION

To prepare intelligently for civil service examinations, you should know how they differ from school examinations you have taken. In school you were assigned certain definite pages to read or subjects to cover. The examination questions were quite detailed and usually emphasized memory. Civil service exams, on the other hand, try to discover your present ability to perform the duties of a position, plus your potentiality to learn these duties. In other words, a civil service exam attempts to predict how successful you will be. Questions cover such a broad area that they cannot be as minute and detailed as school exam questions.

In the public service similar kinds of work, or positions, are grouped together in one "class." This process is known as *position-classification*. All the positions in a class are paid according to the salary range for that class. One class title covers all of these positions, and they are all tested by the same examination.

B. FOUR BASIC STEPS

1) Study the announcement

How, then, can you know what subjects to study? Our best answer is: "Learn as much as possible about the class of positions for which you've applied." The exam will test the knowledge, skills and abilities needed to do the work.

Your most valuable source of information about the position you want is the official exam announcement. This announcement lists the training and experience qualifications. Check these standards and apply only if you come reasonably close to meeting them.

The brief description of the position in the examination announcement offers some clues to the subjects which will be tested. Think about the job itself. Review the duties in your mind. Can you perform them, or are there some in which you are rusty? Fill in the blank spots in your preparation.

Many jurisdictions preview the written test in the exam announcement by including a section called "Knowledge and Abilities Required," "Scope of the Examination," or some similar heading. Here you will find out specifically what fields will be tested.

2) Review your own background

Once you learn in general what the position is all about, and what you need to know to do the work, ask yourself which subjects you already know fairly well and which need improvement. You may wonder whether to concentrate on improving your strong areas or on building some background in your fields of weakness. When the announcement has specified "some knowledge" or "considerable knowledge," or has used adjectives like "beginning principles of…" or "advanced … methods," you can get a clue as to the number and difficulty of questions to be asked in any given field. More questions, and hence broader coverage, would be included for those subjects which are more important in the work. Now weigh your strengths and weaknesses against the job requirements and prepare accordingly.

3) Determine the level of the position

Another way to tell how intensively you should prepare is to understand the level of the job for which you are applying. Is it the entering level? In other words, is this the position in which beginners in a field of work are hired? Or is it an intermediate or advanced level? Sometimes this is indicated by such words as "Junior" or "Senior" in the class title. Other jurisdictions use Roman numerals to designate the level – Clerk I, Clerk II, for example. The word "Supervisor" sometimes appears in the title. If the level is not indicated by the title, check the description of duties. Will you be working under very close supervision, or will you have responsibility for independent decisions in this work?

4) Choose appropriate study materials

Now that you know the subjects to be examined and the relative amount of each subject to be covered, you can choose suitable study materials. For beginning level jobs, or even advanced ones, if you have a pronounced weakness in some aspect of your training, read a modern, standard textbook in that field. Be sure it is up to date and has general coverage. Such books are normally available at your library, and the librarian will be glad to help you locate one. For entry-level positions, questions of appropriate difficulty are chosen – neither highly advanced questions, nor those too simple. Such questions require careful thought but not advanced training.

If the position for which you are applying is technical or advanced, you will read more advanced, specialized material. If you are already familiar with the basic principles of your field, elementary textbooks would waste your time. Concentrate on advanced textbooks and technical periodicals. Think through the concepts and review difficult problems in your field.

These are all general sources. You can get more ideas on your own initiative, following these leads. For example, training manuals and publications of the government agency which employs workers in your field can be useful, particularly for technical and professional positions. A letter or visit to the government department involved may result in more specific study suggestions, and certainly will provide you with a more definite idea of the exact nature of the position you are seeking.

III. KINDS OF TESTS

Tests are used for purposes other than measuring knowledge and ability to perform specified duties. For some positions, it is equally important to test ability to make adjustments to new situations or to profit from training. In others, basic mental abilities not dependent on information are essential. Questions which test these things may not appear as pertinent to the duties of the position as those which test for knowledge and information. Yet they are often highly important parts of a fair examination. For very general questions, it is almost impossible to help you direct your study efforts. What we can do is to point out some of the more common of these general abilities needed in public service positions and describe some typical questions.

1) General information

Broad, general information has been found useful for predicting job success in some kinds of work. This is tested in a variety of ways, from vocabulary lists to questions about current events. Basic background in some field of work, such as sociology or economics, may be sampled in a group of questions. Often these are principles which have become familiar to most persons through exposure rather than through formal training. It is difficult to advise you how to study for these questions; being alert to the world around you is our best suggestion.

2) Verbal ability

An example of an ability needed in many positions is verbal or language ability. Verbal ability is, in brief, the ability to use and understand words. Vocabulary and grammar tests are typical measures of this ability. Reading comprehension or paragraph interpretation questions are common in many kinds of civil service tests. You are given a paragraph of written material and asked to find its central meaning.

3) Numerical ability

Number skills can be tested by the familiar arithmetic problem, by checking paired lists of numbers to see which are alike and which are different, or by interpreting charts and graphs. In the latter test, a graph may be printed in the test booklet which you are asked to use as the basis for answering questions.

4) Observation

A popular test for law-enforcement positions is the observation test. A picture is shown to you for several minutes, then taken away. Questions about the picture test your ability to observe both details and larger elements.

5) Following directions

In many positions in the public service, the employee must be able to carry out written instructions dependably and accurately. You may be given a chart with several columns, each column listing a variety of information. The questions require you to carry out directions involving the information given in the chart.

6) Skills and aptitudes

Performance tests effectively measure some manual skills and aptitudes. When the skill is one in which you are trained, such as typing or shorthand, you can practice. These tests are often very much like those given in business school or high school courses. For many of the other skills and aptitudes, however, no short-time preparation can be made. Skills and abilities natural to you or that you have developed throughout your lifetime are being tested.

Many of the general questions just described provide all the data needed to answer the questions and ask you to use your reasoning ability to find the answers. Your best preparation for these tests, as well as for tests of facts and ideas, is to be at your physical and mental best. You, no doubt, have your own methods of getting into an exam-taking mood and keeping "in shape." The next section lists some ideas on this subject.

IV. KINDS OF QUESTIONS

Only rarely is the "essay" question, which you answer in narrative form, used in civil service tests. Civil service tests are usually of the short-answer type. Full instructions for answering these questions will be given to you at the examination. But in case this is your first experience with short-answer questions and separate answer sheets, here is what you need to know:

1) Multiple-choice Questions

Most popular of the short-answer questions is the "multiple choice" or "best answer" question. It can be used, for example, to test for factual knowledge, ability to solve problems or judgment in meeting situations found at work.

A multiple-choice question is normally one of three types—

- It can begin with an incomplete statement followed by several possible endings. You are to find the one ending which *best* completes the statement, although some of the others may not be entirely wrong.
- It can also be a complete statement in the form of a question which is answered by choosing one of the statements listed.
- It can be in the form of a problem – again you select the best answer.

Here is an example of a multiple-choice question with a discussion which should give you some clues as to the method for choosing the right answer:

When an employee has a complaint about his assignment, the action which will *best* help him overcome his difficulty is to
- A. discuss his difficulty with his coworkers
- B. take the problem to the head of the organization
- C. take the problem to the person who gave him the assignment
- D. say nothing to anyone about his complaint

In answering this question, you should study each of the choices to find which is best. Consider choice "A" – Certainly an employee may discuss his complaint with fellow employees, but no change or improvement can result, and the complaint remains unresolved. Choice "B" is a poor choice since the head of the organization probably does not know what assignment you have been given, and taking your problem to him is known as "going over the head" of the supervisor. The supervisor, or person who made the assignment, is the person who can clarify it or correct any injustice. Choice "C" is, therefore, correct. To say nothing, as in choice "D," is unwise. Supervisors have and interest in knowing the problems employees are facing, and the employee is seeking a solution to his problem.

2) True/False Questions

The "true/false" or "right/wrong" form of question is sometimes used. Here a complete statement is given. Your job is to decide whether the statement is right or wrong.

SAMPLE: A roaming cell-phone call to a nearby city costs less than a non-roaming call to a distant city.

This statement is wrong, or false, since roaming calls are more expensive.

This is not a complete list of all possible question forms, although most of the others are variations of these common types. You will always get complete directions for answering questions. Be sure you understand *how* to mark your answers – ask questions until you do.

V. RECORDING YOUR ANSWERS

Computer terminals are used more and more today for many different kinds of exams.

For an examination with very few applicants, you may be told to record your answers in the test booklet itself. Separate answer sheets are much more common. If this separate answer sheet is to be scored by machine – and this is often the case – it is highly important that you mark your answers correctly in order to get credit.

An electronic scoring machine is often used in civil service offices because of the speed with which papers can be scored. Machine-scored answer sheets must be marked with a pencil, which will be given to you. This pencil has a high graphite content which responds to the electronic scoring machine. As a matter of fact, stray dots may register as answers, so do not let your pencil rest on the answer sheet while you are pondering the correct answer. Also, if your pencil lead breaks or is otherwise defective, ask for another.

Since the answer sheet will be dropped in a slot in the scoring machine, be careful not to bend the corners or get the paper crumpled.

The answer sheet normally has five vertical columns of numbers, with 30 numbers to a column. These numbers correspond to the question numbers in your test booklet. After each number, going across the page are four or five pairs of dotted lines. These short dotted lines have small letters or numbers above them. The first two pairs may also have a "T" or "F" above the letters. This indicates that the first two pairs only are to be used if the questions are of the true-false type. If the questions are multiple choice, disregard the "T" and "F" and pay attention only to the small letters or numbers.

Answer your questions in the manner of the sample that follows:

    32. The largest city in the United States is
        A. Washington, D.C.
        B. New York City
        C. Chicago
        D. Detroit
        E. San Francisco

    1) Choose the answer you think is best. (New York City is the largest, so "B" is
       correct.)
    2) Find the row of dotted lines numbered the same as the question you are
       answering. (Find row number 32)
    3) Find the pair of dotted lines corresponding to the answer. (Find the pair of
       lines under the mark "B.")
    4) Make a solid black mark between the dotted lines.

VI. BEFORE THE TEST

Common sense will help you find procedures to follow to get ready for an examination. Too many of us, however, overlook these sensible measures. Indeed, nervousness and fatigue have been found to be the most serious reasons why applicants fail to do their best on civil service tests. Here is a list of reminders:

- Begin your preparation early – Don't wait until the last minute to go scurrying around for books and materials or to find out what the position is all about.
- Prepare continuously – An hour a night for a week is better than an all-night cram session. This has been definitely established. What is more, a night a week for a month will return better dividends than crowding your study into a shorter period of time.
- Locate the place of the exam – You have been sent a notice telling you when and where to report for the examination. If the location is in a different town or otherwise unfamiliar to you, it would be well to inquire the best route and learn something about the building.
- Relax the night before the test – Allow your mind to rest. Do not study at all that night. Plan some mild recreation or diversion; then go to bed early and get a good night's sleep.
- Get up early enough to make a leisurely trip to the place for the test – This way unforeseen events, traffic snarls, unfamiliar buildings, etc. will not upset you.
- Dress comfortably – A written test is not a fashion show. You will be known by number and not by name, so wear something comfortable.
- Leave excess paraphernalia at home – Shopping bags and odd bundles will get in your way. You need bring only the items mentioned in the official notice you received; usually everything you need is provided. Do not bring reference books to the exam. They will only confuse those last minutes and be taken away from you when in the test room.
- Arrive somewhat ahead of time – If because of transportation schedules you must get there very early, bring a newspaper or magazine to take your mind off yourself while waiting.
- Locate the examination room – When you have found the proper room, you will be directed to the seat or part of the room where you will sit. Sometimes you are given a sheet of instructions to read while you are waiting. Do not fill out any forms until you are told to do so; just read them and be prepared.
- Relax and prepare to listen to the instructions
- If you have any physical problem that may keep you from doing your best, be sure to tell the test administrator. If you are sick or in poor health, you really cannot do your best on the exam. You can come back and take the test some other time.

VII. AT THE TEST

The day of the test is here and you have the test booklet in your hand. The temptation to get going is very strong. Caution! There is more to success than knowing the right answers. You must know how to identify your papers and understand variations in the type of short-answer question used in this particular examination. Follow these suggestions for maximum results from your efforts:

1) Cooperate with the monitor

The test administrator has a duty to create a situation in which you can be as much at ease as possible. He will give instructions, tell you when to begin, check to see that you are marking your answer sheet correctly, and so on. He is not there to guard you, although he will see that your competitors do not take unfair advantage. He wants to help you do your best.

2) Listen to all instructions

Don't jump the gun! Wait until you understand all directions. In most civil service tests you get more time than you need to answer the questions. So don't be in a hurry. Read each word of instructions until you clearly understand the meaning. Study the examples, listen to all announcements and follow directions. Ask questions if you do not understand what to do.

3) Identify your papers

Civil service exams are usually identified by number only. You will be assigned a number; you must not put your name on your test papers. Be sure to copy your number correctly. Since more than one exam may be given, copy your exact examination title.

4) Plan your time

Unless you are told that a test is a "speed" or "rate of work" test, speed itself is usually not important. Time enough to answer all the questions will be provided, but this does not mean that you have all day. An overall time limit has been set. Divide the total time (in minutes) by the number of questions to determine the approximate time you have for each question.

5) Do not linger over difficult questions

If you come across a difficult question, mark it with a paper clip (useful to have along) and come back to it when you have been through the booklet. One caution if you do this – be sure to skip a number on your answer sheet as well. Check often to be sure that you have not lost your place and that you are marking in the row numbered the same as the question you are answering.

6) Read the questions

Be sure you know what the question asks! Many capable people are unsuccessful because they failed to *read* the questions correctly.

7) Answer all questions

Unless you have been instructed that a penalty will be deducted for incorrect answers, it is better to guess than to omit a question.

8) Speed tests

It is often better NOT to guess on speed tests. It has been found that on timed tests people are tempted to spend the last few seconds before time is called in marking answers at random – without even reading them – in the hope of picking up a few extra points. To discourage this practice, the instructions may warn you that your score will be "corrected" for guessing. That is, a penalty will be applied. The incorrect answers will be deducted from the correct ones, or some other penalty formula will be used.

9) Review your answers

      If you finish before time is called, go back to the questions you guessed or omitted to give them further thought. Review other answers if you have time.

10) Return your test materials

      If you are ready to leave before others have finished or time is called, take ALL your materials to the monitor and leave quietly. Never take any test material with you. The monitor can discover whose papers are not complete, and taking a test booklet may be grounds for disqualification.

VIII. EXAMINATION TECHNIQUES

1) Read the general instructions carefully. These are usually printed on the first page of the exam booklet. As a rule, these instructions refer to the timing of the examination; the fact that you should not start work until the signal and must stop work at a signal, etc. If there are any *special* instructions, such as a choice of questions to be answered, make sure that you note this instruction carefully.

2) When you are ready to start work on the examination, that is as soon as the signal has been given, read the instructions to each question booklet, underline any key words or phrases, such as *least, best, outline, describe* and the like. In this way you will tend to answer as requested rather than discover on reviewing your paper that you *listed without describing*, that you selected the *worst* choice rather than the *best* choice, etc.

3) If the examination is of the objective or multiple-choice type – that is, each question will also give a series of possible answers: A, B, C or D, and you are called upon to select the best answer and write the letter next to that answer on your answer paper – it is advisable to start answering each question in turn. There may be anywhere from 50 to 100 such questions in the three or four hours allotted and you can see how much time would be taken if you read through all the questions before beginning to answer any. Furthermore, if you come across a question or group of questions which you know would be difficult to answer, it would undoubtedly affect your handling of all the other questions.

4) If the examination is of the essay type and contains but a few questions, it is a moot point as to whether you should read all the questions before starting to answer any one. Of course, if you are given a choice – say five out of seven and the like – then it is essential to read all the questions so you can eliminate the two that are most difficult. If, however, you are asked to answer all the questions, there may be danger in trying to answer the easiest one first because you may find that you will spend too much time on it. The best technique is to answer the first question, then proceed to the second, etc.

5) Time your answers. Before the exam begins, write down the time it started, then add the time allowed for the examination and write down the time it must be completed, then divide the time available somewhat as follows:

- If 3-1/2 hours are allowed, that would be 210 minutes. If you have 80 objective-type questions, that would be an average of 2-1/2 minutes per question. Allow yourself no more than 2 minutes per question, or a total of 160 minutes, which will permit about 50 minutes to review.
- If for the time allotment of 210 minutes there are 7 essay questions to answer, that would average about 30 minutes a question. Give yourself only 25 minutes per question so that you have about 35 minutes to review.

6) The most important instruction is to *read each question* and make sure you know what is wanted. The second most important instruction is to *time yourself properly* so that you answer every question. The third most important instruction is to *answer every question.* Guess if you have to but include something for each question. Remember that you will receive no credit for a blank and will probably receive some credit if you write something in answer to an essay question. If you guess a letter – say "B" for a multiple-choice question – you may have guessed right. If you leave a blank as an answer to a multiple-choice question, the examiners may respect your feelings but it will not add a point to your score. Some exams may penalize you for wrong answers, so in such cases *only,* you may not want to guess unless you have some basis for your answer.

7) Suggestions
   a. Objective-type questions
      1. Examine the question booklet for proper sequence of pages and questions
      2. Read all instructions carefully
      3. Skip any question which seems too difficult; return to it after all other questions have been answered
      4. Apportion your time properly; do not spend too much time on any single question or group of questions
      5. Note and underline key words – *all, most, fewest, least, best, worst, same, opposite,* etc.
      6. Pay particular attention to negatives
      7. Note unusual option, e.g., unduly long, short, complex, different or similar in content to the body of the question
      8. Observe the use of "hedging" words – *probably, may, most likely,* etc.
      9. Make sure that your answer is put next to the same number as the question
      10. Do not second-guess unless you have good reason to believe the second answer is definitely more correct
      11. Cross out original answer if you decide another answer is more accurate; do not erase until you are ready to hand your paper in
      12. Answer all questions; guess unless instructed otherwise
      13. Leave time for review

   b. Essay questions
      1. Read each question carefully
      2. Determine exactly what is wanted. Underline key words or phrases.
      3. Decide on outline or paragraph answer

4. Include many different points and elements unless asked to develop any one or two points or elements
5. Show impartiality by giving pros and cons unless directed to select one side only
6. Make and write down any assumptions you find necessary to answer the questions
7. Watch your English, grammar, punctuation and choice of words
8. Time your answers; don't crowd material

8) Answering the essay question

Most essay questions can be answered by framing the specific response around several key words or ideas. Here are a few such key words or ideas:

M's: manpower, materials, methods, money, management
P's: purpose, program, policy, plan, procedure, practice, problems, pitfalls, personnel, public relations
   a. Six basic steps in handling problems:
       1. Preliminary plan and background development
       2. Collect information, data and facts
       3. Analyze and interpret information, data and facts
       4. Analyze and develop solutions as well as make recommendations
       5. Prepare report and sell recommendations
       6. Install recommendations and follow up effectiveness

   b. Pitfalls to avoid
       1. *Taking things for granted* – A statement of the situation does not necessarily imply that each of the elements is necessarily true; for example, a complaint may be invalid and biased so that all that can be taken for granted is that a complaint has been registered
       2. *Considering only one side of a situation* – Wherever possible, indicate several alternatives and then point out the reasons you selected the best one
       3. *Failing to indicate follow up* – Whenever your answer indicates action on your part, make certain that you will take proper follow-up action to see how successful your recommendations, procedures or actions turn out to be
       4. *Taking too long in answering any single question* – Remember to time your answers properly

IX. AFTER THE TEST

Scoring procedures differ in detail among civil service jurisdictions although the general principles are the same. Whether the papers are hand-scored or graded by machine we have described, they are nearly always graded by number. That is, the person who marks the paper knows only the number – never the name – of the applicant. Not until all the papers have been graded will they be matched with names. If other tests, such as training and experience or oral interview ratings have been given, scores will be combined. Different parts of the examination usually have different weights. For example, the written test might count 60 percent of the final grade, and a rating of training and experience 40 percent. In many jurisdictions, veterans will have a certain number of points added to their grades.

After the final grade has been determined, the names are placed in grade order and an eligible list is established. There are various methods for resolving ties between those who get the same final grade – probably the most common is to place first the name of the person whose application was received first. Job offers are made from the eligible list in the order the names appear on it. You will be notified of your grade and your rank as soon as all these computations have been made. This will be done as rapidly as possible.

People who are found to meet the requirements in the announcement are called "eligibles." Their names are put on a list of eligible candidates. An eligible's chances of getting a job depend on how high he stands on this list and how fast agencies are filling jobs from the list.

When a job is to be filled from a list of eligibles, the agency asks for the names of people on the list of eligibles for that job. When the civil service commission receives this request, it sends to the agency the names of the three people highest on this list. Or, if the job to be filled has specialized requirements, the office sends the agency the names of the top three persons who meet these requirements from the general list.

The appointing officer makes a choice from among the three people whose names were sent to him. If the selected person accepts the appointment, the names of the others are put back on the list to be considered for future openings.

That is the rule in hiring from all kinds of eligible lists, whether they are for typist, carpenter, chemist, or something else. For every vacancy, the appointing officer has his choice of any one of the top three eligibles on the list. This explains why the person whose name is on top of the list sometimes does not get an appointment when some of the persons lower on the list do. If the appointing officer chooses the second or third eligible, the No. 1 eligible does not get a job at once, but stays on the list until he is appointed or the list is terminated.

X. HOW TO PASS THE INTERVIEW TEST

The examination for which you applied requires an oral interview test. You have already taken the written test and you are now being called for the interview test – the final part of the formal examination.

You may think that it is not possible to prepare for an interview test and that there are no procedures to follow during an interview. Our purpose is to point out some things you can do in advance that will help you and some good rules to follow and pitfalls to avoid while you are being interviewed.

What is an interview supposed to test?
The written examination is designed to test the technical knowledge and competence of the candidate; the oral is designed to evaluate intangible qualities, not readily measured otherwise, and to establish a list showing the relative fitness of each candidate – as measured against his competitors – for the position sought. Scoring is not on the basis of "right" and "wrong," but on a sliding scale of values ranging from "not passable" to "outstanding." As a matter of fact, it is possible to achieve a relatively low score without a single "incorrect" answer because of evident weakness in the qualities being measured.

Occasionally, an examination may consist entirely of an oral test – either an individual or a group oral. In such cases, information is sought concerning the technical knowledges and abilities of the candidate, since there has been no written examination for this purpose. More commonly, however, an oral test is used to supplement a written examination.

Who conducts interviews?

The composition of oral boards varies among different jurisdictions. In nearly all, a representative of the personnel department serves as chairman. One of the members of the board may be a representative of the department in which the candidate would work. In some cases, "outside experts" are used, and, frequently, a businessman or some other representative of the general public is asked to serve. Labor and management or other special groups may be represented. The aim is to secure the services of experts in the appropriate field.

However the board is composed, it is a good idea (and not at all improper or unethical) to ascertain in advance of the interview who the members are and what groups they represent. When you are introduced to them, you will have some idea of their backgrounds and interests, and at least you will not stutter and stammer over their names.

What should be done before the interview?

While knowledge about the board members is useful and takes some of the surprise element out of the interview, there is other preparation which is more substantive. It *is* possible to prepare for an oral interview – in several ways:

1) Keep a copy of your application and review it carefully before the interview

This may be the only document before the oral board, and the starting point of the interview. Know what education and experience you have listed there, and the sequence and dates of all of it. Sometimes the board will ask you to review the highlights of your experience for them; you should not have to hem and haw doing it.

2) Study the class specification and the examination announcement

Usually, the oral board has one or both of these to guide them. The qualities, characteristics or knowledges required by the position sought are stated in these documents. They offer valuable clues as to the nature of the oral interview. For example, if the job involves supervisory responsibilities, the announcement will usually indicate that knowledge of modern supervisory methods and the qualifications of the candidate as a supervisor will be tested. If so, you can expect such questions, frequently in the form of a hypothetical situation which you are expected to solve. NEVER go into an oral without knowledge of the duties and responsibilities of the job you seek.

3) Think through each qualification required

Try to visualize the kind of questions you would ask if you were a board member. How well could you answer them? Try especially to appraise your own knowledge and background in each area, *measured against the job sought*, and identify any areas in which you are weak. Be critical and realistic – do not flatter yourself.

4) Do some general reading in areas in which you feel you may be weak

For example, if the job involves supervision and your past experience has NOT, some general reading in supervisory methods and practices, particularly in the field of human relations, might be useful. Do NOT study agency procedures or detailed manuals. The oral board will be testing your understanding and capacity, not your memory.

5) Get a good night's sleep and watch your general health and mental attitude

You will want a clear head at the interview. Take care of a cold or any other minor ailment, and of course, no hangovers.

What should be done on the day of the interview?

Now comes the day of the interview itself. Give yourself plenty of time to get there. Plan to arrive somewhat ahead of the scheduled time, particularly if your appointment is in the fore part of the day. If a previous candidate fails to appear, the board might be ready for you a bit early. By early afternoon an oral board is almost invariably behind schedule if there are many candidates, and you may have to wait. Take along a book or magazine to read, or your application to review, but leave any extraneous material in the waiting room when you go in for your interview. In any event, relax and compose yourself.

The matter of dress is important. The board is forming impressions about you – from your experience, your manners, your attitude, and your appearance. Give your personal appearance careful attention. Dress your best, but not your flashiest. Choose conservative, appropriate clothing, and be sure it is immaculate. This is a business interview, and your appearance should indicate that you regard it as such. Besides, being well groomed and properly dressed will help boost your confidence.

Sooner or later, someone will call your name and escort you into the interview room. *This is it.* From here on you are on your own. It is too late for any more preparation. But remember, you asked for this opportunity to prove your fitness, and you are here because your request was granted.

What happens when you go in?

The usual sequence of events will be as follows: The clerk (who is often the board stenographer) will introduce you to the chairman of the oral board, who will introduce you to the other members of the board. Acknowledge the introductions before you sit down. Do not be surprised if you find a microphone facing you or a stenotypist sitting by. Oral interviews are usually recorded in the event of an appeal or other review.

Usually the chairman of the board will open the interview by reviewing the highlights of your education and work experience from your application – primarily for the benefit of the other members of the board, as well as to get the material into the record. Do not interrupt or comment unless there is an error or significant misinterpretation; if that is the case, do not hesitate. But do not quibble about insignificant matters. Also, he will usually ask you some question about your education, experience or your present job – partly to get you to start talking and to establish the interviewing "rapport." He may start the actual questioning, or turn it over to one of the other members. Frequently, each member undertakes the questioning on a particular area, one in which he is perhaps most competent, so you can expect each member to participate in the examination. Because time is limited, you may also expect some rather abrupt switches in the direction the questioning takes, so do not be upset by it. Normally, a board member will not pursue a single line of questioning unless he discovers a particular strength or weakness.

After each member has participated, the chairman will usually ask whether any member has any further questions, then will ask you if you have anything you wish to add. Unless you are expecting this question, it may floor you. Worse, it may start you off on an extended, extemporaneous speech. The board is not usually seeking more information. The question is principally to offer you a last opportunity to present further qualifications or to indicate that you have nothing to add. So, if you feel that a significant qualification or characteristic has been overlooked, it is proper to point it out in a sentence or so. Do not compliment the board on the thoroughness of their examination – they have been sketchy, and you know it. If you wish, merely say, "No thank you, I have nothing further to add." This is a point where you can "talk yourself out" of a good impression or fail to present an important bit of information. Remember, *you close the interview yourself.*

The chairman will then say, "That is all, Mr. _____, thank you." Do not be startled; the interview is over, and quicker than you think. Thank him, gather your belongings and take your leave. Save your sigh of relief for the other side of the door.

How to put your best foot forward

Throughout this entire process, you may feel that the board individually and collectively is trying to pierce your defenses, seek out your hidden weaknesses and embarrass and confuse you. Actually, this is not true. They are obliged to make an appraisal of your qualifications for the job you are seeking, and they want to see you in your best light. Remember, they must interview all candidates and a non-cooperative candidate may become a failure in spite of their best efforts to bring out his qualifications. Here are 15 suggestions that will help you:

1) Be natural – Keep your attitude confident, not cocky

If you are not confident that you can do the job, do not expect the board to be. Do not apologize for your weaknesses, try to bring out your strong points. The board is interested in a positive, not negative, presentation. Cockiness will antagonize any board member and make him wonder if you are covering up a weakness by a false show of strength.

2) Get comfortable, but don't lounge or sprawl

Sit erectly but not stiffly. A careless posture may lead the board to conclude that you are careless in other things, or at least that you are not impressed by the importance of the occasion. Either conclusion is natural, even if incorrect. Do not fuss with your clothing, a pencil or an ashtray. Your hands may occasionally be useful to emphasize a point; do not let them become a point of distraction.

3) Do not wisecrack or make small talk

This is a serious situation, and your attitude should show that you consider it as such. Further, the time of the board is limited – they do not want to waste it, and neither should you.

4) Do not exaggerate your experience or abilities

In the first place, from information in the application or other interviews and sources, the board may know more about you than you think. Secondly, you probably will not get away with it. An experienced board is rather adept at spotting such a situation, so do not take the chance.

5) If you know a board member, do not make a point of it, yet do not hide it

Certainly you are not fooling him, and probably not the other members of the board. Do not try to take advantage of your acquaintanceship – it will probably do you little good.

6) Do not dominate the interview

Let the board do that. They will give you the clues – do not assume that you have to do all the talking. Realize that the board has a number of questions to ask you, and do not try to take up all the interview time by showing off your extensive knowledge of the answer to the first one.

7) Be attentive

You only have 20 minutes or so, and you should keep your attention at its sharpest throughout. When a member is addressing a problem or question to you, give him your undivided attention. Address your reply principally to him, but do not exclude the other board members.

8) Do not interrupt

A board member may be stating a problem for you to analyze. He will ask you a question when the time comes. Let him state the problem, and wait for the question.

9) Make sure you understand the question

Do not try to answer until you are sure what the question is. If it is not clear, restate it in your own words or ask the board member to clarify it for you. However, do not haggle about minor elements.

10) Reply promptly but not hastily

A common entry on oral board rating sheets is "candidate responded readily," or "candidate hesitated in replies." Respond as promptly and quickly as you can, but do not jump to a hasty, ill-considered answer.

11) Do not be peremptory in your answers

A brief answer is proper – but do not fire your answer back. That is a losing game from your point of view. The board member can probably ask questions much faster than you can answer them.

12) Do not try to create the answer you think the board member wants

He is interested in what kind of mind you have and how it works – not in playing games. Furthermore, he can usually spot this practice and will actually grade you down on it.

13) Do not switch sides in your reply merely to agree with a board member

Frequently, a member will take a contrary position merely to draw you out and to see if you are willing and able to defend your point of view. Do not start a debate, yet do not surrender a good position. If a position is worth taking, it is worth defending.

14) Do not be afraid to admit an error in judgment if you are shown to be wrong

The board knows that you are forced to reply without any opportunity for careful consideration. Your answer may be demonstrably wrong. If so, admit it and get on with the interview.

15) Do not dwell at length on your present job

The opening question may relate to your present assignment. Answer the question but do not go into an extended discussion. You are being examined for a *new* job, not your present one. As a matter of fact, try to phrase ALL your answers in terms of the job for which you are being examined.

Basis of Rating

Probably you will forget most of these "do's" and "don'ts" when you walk into the oral interview room. Even remembering them all will not ensure you a passing grade. Perhaps you did not have the qualifications in the first place. But remembering them will help you to put your best foot forward, without treading on the toes of the board members.

Rumor and popular opinion to the contrary notwithstanding, an oral board wants you to make the best appearance possible. They know you are under pressure – but they also want to see how you respond to it as a guide to what your reaction would be under the pressures of the job you seek. They will be influenced by the degree of poise you display, the personal traits you show and the manner in which you respond.

ABOUT THIS BOOK

This book contains tests divided into Examination Sections. Go through each test, answering every question in the margin. At the end of each test look at the answer key and check your answers. On the ones you got wrong, look at the right answer choice and learn. Do not fill in the answers first. Do not memorize the questions and answers, but understand the answer and principles involved. On your test, the questions will likely be different from the samples. Questions are changed and new ones added. If you understand these past questions you should have success with any changes that arise. Tests may consist of several types of questions. We have additional books on each subject should more study be advisable or necessary for you. Finally, the more you study, the better prepared you will be. This book is intended to be the last thing you study before you walk into the examination room. Prior study of relevant texts is also recommended. NLC publishes some of these in our Fundamental Series. Knowledge and good sense are important factors in passing your exam. Good luck also helps. So now study this Passbook, absorb the material contained within and take that knowledge into the examination. Then do your best to pass that exam.

———

EXAMINATION SECTION

EXAMINATION SECTION
TEST 1

DIRECTIONS: Each question or incomplete statement is followed by several suggested answers or completions. Select the one that BEST answers the question or completes the statement. *PRINT THE LETTER OF THE CORRECT ANSWER IN THE SPACE AT THE RIGHT.*

1. A certain system for handling office supplies requires that supplies be issued to the various agency offices only on a bi-weekly basis and that all supply requisitions be authorized by the unit supervisor.
The BEST reason for establishing this supplies system is to

   A. standardize ordering descriptions and stock identification codes
   B. prevent the disordering of stock shelves and cabinets by unauthorized persons searching for supplies
   C. ensure that unit supervisors properly exercise their right to make determinations on supply orders
   D. encourage proper utilization of supplies to control the workload

   1.____

2. It is important that every office have a retention and disposal program for filing material. Suppose that you have been appointed administrative assistant in an office with a poorly organized records-retention program.
In establishing a revised program for the transfer or disposal of records, the step which would logically be taken THIRD in the process is

   A. preparing a safe and inexpensive storage area and setting up an indexing system for records already in storage
   B. determining what papers to retain and for how long a period
   C. taking an inventory of what is filed, where it is filed, how much is filed, and how often it is used
   D. moving records from active to inactive files and destroying useless records

   2.____

3. In the effective design of office forms, the FIRST step to take is to

   A. decide what information should be included
   B. decide the purpose for which the form will be used
   C. identify the form by name and number
   D. identify the employees who will be using the form

   3.____

4. Some designers of office forms prefer to locate the instructions on how to fill out the form at the bottom of it. The MOST logical objection to placing such instructions at the bottom of the form is that

   A. instructions at the bottom require an excess of space
   B. all form instructions should be outlined with a separate paragraph
   C. the form may be partly filled out before the instructions are seen
   D. the bottom of the form should be reserved only for authorization and signature

   4.____

5. A formal business report may consist of many parts, including the following:　　　　5.＿＿＿
     I.   Table of contents
     II. List of references
     III. Preface
     IV. Index
     V. List of tables
     VI. Conclusions or recommendations
Of the following, in setting up a formal report, the PROPER order of the six parts listed is

    A. I, III, VI, V, II, IV   B. IV, III, II, V, VI, I
    C. III, I, V, VI, II, IV   D. II, V, III, I, IV, VI

6. Three of the basic functions of office management are considered to be planning, con-　　6.＿＿＿
trolling, and organizing. Of the following, the one which might BEST be considered
ORGANIZING activity is

    A. assigning personnel and materials to work units to achieve agreed-upon objectives
    B. determining future objectives and indicating conditions affecting the accomplishment of the goals
    C. evaluating accomplishments and applying necessary corrective measures to insure results
    D. motivating employees to perform their work in accordance with objectives

7. The following four statements relate to office layout.　　7.＿＿＿
     I.   Position supervisors' desks at the front of their work group so that they can easily be recognized as persons in authority
     II. Arrange file cabinets and frequently used equipment near the employees who utilize them most often
     III. Locate the receptionist's desk near the entrance of the office so that visitor traffic will not distract other workers
     IV. Divide a large office area into many smaller offices by using stationary partitions so that all employees may have privacy and prestige
According to authorities in office management and administration, which of these
statements are GENERALLY recommended guides to effective office layout?

    A. I, II, III   B. II, III, IV
    C. II, III   D. All of the above

8. For which of the following purposes would a flow chart have the GREATEST applicabil-　　8.＿＿＿
ity?

    A. Training new employees in performance of routinized duties
    B. Determining adequacy of performance of employees
    C. Determining the accuracy of the organization chart
    D. Locating causes of delays in carrying out an operation

9. Office work management concerns tangible accomplishment or production. It has to do　　9.＿＿＿
with results; it does not deal with the amount of energy expended by the individual who
produces the results.
According to this statement, the production in which of the following kinds of jobs
would be MOST difficult to measure accurately? A(n)

A. file clerk
B. secretary
C. computer operator
D. office administrator

10. The FIRST step in the statistical analysis of a great mass of data secured from a survey is to

    A. scan the data to determine which is atypical of the survey
    B. determine the number of deviations from the average
    C. arrange the data into groups on the basis of likenesses and differences
    D. plot the data on a graph to determine trends

10.____

11. Suppose that, as an administrative assistant in charge of an office, you are required to change the layout of your office to accommodate expanding functions.
    The LEAST important factor to be considered in planning the revised layout is the

    A. relative productivity of individuals in the office
    B. communication and work flow needs
    C. need for screening confidential activities from unauthorized persons
    D. areas of noise concentration

11.____

12. Suppose you have instructed a new employee to follow a standardized series of steps to accomplish a job. He is to use a rubber stamp, then a red pencil on the first paper, and a numbering machine on the second. Then, he is to staple the two sheets of paper together and put them to one side. You observe, however, that he sometimes uses the red pencil first, sometimes the numbering machine first. At other times, he does the stapling before using the numbering machine.
    For you as supervisor to suggest that the clerk use the standardized method when doing this job would be

    A. *bad,* because the clerk should be given a chance to use his independent judgment on the best way to do his job
    B. *good,* because the clerk's sequence of actions results in a loss of efficiency
    C. *bad,* because it is not wise to interrupt the work habit the clerk has already developed
    D. *good,* because the clerk should not be permitted to make unauthorized changes in standard office routines

12.____

13. Suppose study of the current records management system for students' transcripts reveals needless recopying of transcript data throughout various offices within the university. On this basis, a recommendation is made that this unnecessary recopying of information be eliminated.
    This decision to eliminate waste in material, time, and space is an application of the office management principle of

    A. work simplification
    B. routing and scheduling
    C. job analysis
    D. cost and budgetary control

13.____

14. It is generally LEAST practical for an office manager to prepare for known peak work periods by

    A. putting job procedures into writing so that they can be handled by more than one person
    B. arranging to make assignments of work on a short-interval scheduling basis

14.____

C. cleaning up as much work as possible ahead of known peak periods
D. rotating jobs and assignments among different employees to assure staff flexibility

15. The four statements below are about office manuals used for various purposes. 15.____
If you had the job of designing and controlling several kinds of office manuals to be used in your agency, which one of these statements would BEST apply as a general rule for you to follow?

    A. Office manual content should be classified into main topics with proper subdivisions arranged in strict alphabetical order.
    B. Manual additions and revisions should be distributed promptly to all holders of manuals for their approval, correction, and criticism.
    C. The language used in office manuals should be simple, and charts and diagrams should be interspersed within the narrative material for further clarity.
    D. Office manual content should be classified into main topics arranged in strict alphabetical order with subtopics in sequence according to importance.

16. Suppose that, as an administrative assistant, you have been assigned to plan the reorga- 16.____
nization of an office which has not been operating efficiently because of the uncoordinated manner in which new functions have been assigned to it over the past year.
The FIRST thing you should do is

    A. call a meeting of the office staff and explain the purposes of the planned reorganization
    B. make a cost-value analysis of the present operations to determine what should be changed or eliminated
    C. prepare a diagram of the flow of work as you think it should be
    D. define carefully the current objectives to be achieved by this reorganization

17. Effective organization requires that specific actions be taken in proper sequence. 17.____
The following are four actions essential to effective organization:
    I. Group activities on the basis of human and material resources
    II. Coordinate functions and provide for good communications
    III. Formulate objectives, policies, and plans
    IV. Determine activities necessary to accomplish goals
The PROPER sequence of these four actions is:

    A. III, II, IV, I   B. IV, III, I, II
    C. III, IV, I, II   D. IV, I, III, II

18. For an administrative assistant to give each of his subordinates exactly the same type of 18.____
supervision is

    A. *advisable,* because he will gain a reputation for being fair and impartial
    B. *inadvisable,* because subordinates work more diligently when they think they are receiving preferential treatment
    C. *advisable,* because most human problems can be classified into categories which make them easier to handle
    D. *inadvisable,* because people differ and there is no one supervisory procedure that applies in every case to dealing with individuals

19. Suppose that, as an administrative assistant, you find that some of your subordinates are coming to you with complaints you think are trivial.
For you to hear them through is

    A. *poor practice*; subordinates should be trained to come to you only with major grievances
    B. *good practice*; major grievances sometimes are the underlying cause of minor complaints
    C. *poor practice*; you should delegate this kind of matter and spend your time on more important problems
    D. *good practice*; this will make you more popular with your subordinates

19._____

20. Suppose that a new departmental policy has just been established which you feel may be resented by your subordinates, but which they must understand and follow. Which would it be most advisable for you as their supervisor to do FIRST?

    A. Make clear to your subordinates that you are not responsible for making this policy.
    B. Tell your subordinates that you agree with the policy whether you do or not.
    C. Explain specifically to your subordinates the reasons for the policy and how it is going to affect them.
    D. Distribute a memo outlining the new policy and require your subordinates to read it.

20._____

21. An office assistant under your supervision tells you that she is reluctant to speak to one of her subordinates about poor work habits because this subordinate is strong-willed, and she does not want to antagonize her.
For you to refuse the office assistant's request that you speak to her subordinate about this matter is

    A. *inadvisable,* since you are in a position of greater authority
    B. *advisable,* since supervision of this subordinate is a basic responsibility of that office assistant
    C. *inadvisable,* since the office assistant must work more closely with her subordinate than you do
    D. *advisable,* since you should not risk antagonizing her subordinate yourself

21._____

22. The GREATEST advantage to a supervisor of using oral communications as compared to written is the

    A. opportunity provided for immediate feedback
    B. speed with which orders can be given and carried out
    C. reduction in amount of paper work
    D. establishment of an informal atmosphere

22._____

23. Of the following, the MOST important reason for an administrative assistant to have private, face-to-face discussions with subordinates about their performance is

    A. encourage a more competitive spirit among employees
    B. give special praise to employees who perform well
    C. discipline employees who perform poorly
    D. help employees improve their work

23._____

24. For a supervisor to keep records of reprimands to subordinates about violations of rules is   24._____

    A. *poor practice*; such records are evidence of the supervisor's inability to maintain discipline
    B. *good practice*; these records are valuable to support disciplinary actions recommended or taken
    C. *poor practice*; the best way to prevent recurrences is to apply penalties without delay
    D. *good practice*; such records are evidence that the supervisor is doing a good job

25. As an administrative assistant supervising a small office, you decide to hold a staff meeting to try to find an acceptable solution to a problem that is causing serious conflicts within the group.
At this meeting, your role should be to present the problem and   25._____

    A. see that the group keeps the problem in focus and does not discuss irrelevant matters
    B. act as chairman of the meeting, but take no other part in the discussion
    C. see to it that each member of the group offers a suggestion for its solution
    D. state your views on the matter before any discussion gets under way

---

KEY (CORRECT ANSWERS)

1. D			11. A	
2. A			12. B	
3. B			13. A	
4. C			14. B	
5. C			15. C	
6. A			16. D	
7. C			17. C	
8. D			18. D	
9. D			19. B	
10. C			20. C	

21. B
22. A
23. D
24. B
25. A

TEST 2

DIRECTIONS: Each question or incomplete statement is followed by several suggested answers or completions. Select the one that BEST answers the question or completes the statement. *PRINT THE LETTER OF THE CORRECT ANSWER IN THE SPACE AT THE RIGHT.*

1. Suppose that one of your subordinates who supervises two young office assistants has been late for work a number of times and you have decided to talk to him about it. In your discussion, it would be MOST constructive for you to emphasize that

    A. personal problems cannot be used as an excuse for these latenesses
    B. the department suffers financially when he is late
    C. you will be forced to give him a less desirable assignment if his latenesses continue
    D. his latenesses set a bad example to those he supervises

1.____

2. Suppose that, as a newly-appointed administrative assistant, you are in charge of a small but very busy office. Your four subordinates are often required to make quick decisions on a wide range of matters while answering telephone or in-person inquiries. You can MOST efficiently help your subordinates meet such situations by

    A. delegating authority to make such decisions to only one or two trusted subordinates
    B. training each subordinate in the proper response for each kind of inquiry that might be made
    C. making certain that subordinates understand clearly the basic policies that affect these decisions
    D. making each subordinate an expert in one area

2.____

3. Of the following, the MOST recent development in methods of training supervisors that involves the human relations approach is

    A. conference training   B. the lecture method
    C. the case method   D. sensitivity training

3.____

4. Which of the following is MOST likely to result in failure as a supervisor?

    A. Showing permissiveness in relations with subordinates
    B. Avoiding delegation of tasks to subordinates
    C. Setting high performance standards for subordinates
    D. Using discipline only when necessary

4.____

5. The MOST important long-range benefit to an organization of proper delegation of work by supervisors is *generally* that

    A. subordinates will be developed to assume greater responsibilities
    B. subordinates will perform the work as their supervisors would
    C. errors in delegated work will be eliminated
    D. more efficient communication among organizational components will result

5.____

6. Which of the following duties would it be LEAST appropriate for an administrative assistant in charge of an office to delegate to an immediate subordinate?   6.____

   A. Checking of figures to be used in a report to the head of the department
   B. On-the-job training of newly appointed college office assistants
   C. Reorganization of assignments for higher level office staff
   D. Contacting other school offices for needed information

7. Decisions should be delegated to the lowest point in the organization at which they can be made effectively.   7.____
The one of the following which is MOST likely to be a result of the application of this accepted management principle is that

   A. upward communications will be facilitated
   B. potential for more rapid decisions and implementation is increased
   C. coordination of decisions that are made will be simplified
   D. no important factors will be overlooked in making decisions

8. The lecture-demonstration method would be LEAST desirable in a training program set up for   8.____

   A. changing the attitudes of long-term employees
   B. informing subordinates about new procedures
   C. explaining how a new office machine works
   D. orientation of new employees

9. Which one of the following conditions would be LEAST likely to indicate a need for employee training?   9.____

   A. Large number of employee suggestions
   B. Large amount of overtime
   C. High number of chronic latenesses
   D. Low employee morale

10. An administrative assistant is planning to make a recommendation to change a procedure which would substantially affect the work of his subordinates.   10.____
For this supervisor to consult with his subordinates about the recommendation before sending it through would be

   A. *undesirable*; subordinates may lose respect for a supervisor who evidences such indecisiveness
   B. *desirable;* since the change in procedure would affect their work, subordinates should decide whether the change should be made
   C. *undesirable;* since subordinates would not receive credit if the procedure were changed, their morale would be lowered
   D. *desirable;* the subordinates may have some worthwhile suggestions concerning the recommendation

11. The BEST way to measure improvement in a selected group of office assistants who have undergone a training course in the use of specific techniques is to   11.____

   A. have the trainees fill out questionnaires at the completion of the course as to what they have learned and giving their opinions as to the value of the course

B. compare the performance of the trainees who completed the course with the performance of office assistants who did not take the course
C. compare the performance of the trainees in these techniques before and after the training course
D. compare the degree of success on the next promotion examination of trainees and non-trainees

12. When an administrative assistant finds it necessary to call in a subordinate for a disciplinary interview, his MAIN objective should be to   12._____

    A. use techniques which can penetrate any deception and get at the truth
    B. stress correction of, rather than punishment for, past errors
    C. maintain a reputation for being an understanding superior
    D. decide on disciplinary action that is consistent with penalties applied for similar infractions

13. Suppose that a newly promoted office assistant does satisfactory work during the first five months of her probationary period. However, her supervisor notices shortly after this time that her performance is falling below acceptable standards. The supervisor decides to keep records of this employee's performance, and if there is no significant improvement by the end of 11 months, to recommend that this employee not be given tenure in the higher title.   13._____
This, as the sole course of action, is

    A. *justified;* employees who do not perform satisfactorily should not be promoted
    B. *unjustified;* the supervisor should attempt to determine the cause of the poor performance as soon as possible
    C. *justified;* the supervisor will have given the subordinate the full probationary period to improve herself
    D. *unjustified;* the subordinate should be demoted to her previous title as soon as her work becomes unsatisfactory

14. Suppose that you are conducting a conference-style training course for a group of 12 office assistants. Miss Jones is the only conferee who has not become involved in the discussion.   14._____
The BEST method of getting Miss Jones to participate is to

    A. ask her to comment on remarks made by the best-informed participant
    B. ask her to give a brief talk at the next session on a topic that interests her
    C. set up a role-play situation and assign her to take a part
    D. ask her a direct question which you know she can answer

15. Which of the following is NOT part of the *control* function of office management?   15._____

    A. Deciding on alternative courses of action
    B. Reporting periodically on productivity
    C. Evaluating performance against the standards
    D. Correcting deviations when required

16. Which of the following is NOT a principal aspect of the process of delegation?   16._____

    A. Developing improvements in methods used to carry out assignments
    B. Granting of permission to do what is necessary to carry out assignments

C. Assignment of duties by a supervisor to an immediate subordinate
D. Obligation on the part of a subordinate to carry out his assignment

17. Reluctance of a supervisor to delegate work effectively may be due to any or all of the following EXCEPT the supervisor's   17.____

    A. unwillingness to take calculated risks
    B. lack of confidence in subordinates
    C. inability to give proper directions as to what he wants done
    D. retention of ultimate responsibility for delegated work

18. A man cannot serve two masters.   18.____
This statement emphasizes the importance in an organization of following the principle of

    A. specialization of work
    B. unity of command
    C. uniformity of assignment
    D. span of control

19. In general, the number of subordinates an administrative assistant can supervise effectively tends to vary   19.____

    A. *directly* with both similarity and complexity of their duties
    B. *directly* with similarity of their duties and *inversely* with complexity of their duties
    C. *inversely* with both similarity and complexity of their duties
    D. *inversely* with similarity of their duties and *directly* with complexity of their duties

20. When an administrative assistant practices *general* rather than *close* supervision, which one of the following is MOST likely to happen?   20.____

    A. His subordinates will not be as well-trained as employees who are supervised more closely.
    B. Standards are likely to be lowered because subordinates will be under fewer pressures and will not be motivated to work toward set goals.
    C. He will give fewer specific orders and spend more time on planning and coordinating than those supervisors who practice close supervision.
    D. This supervisor will spend more time checking and correcting mistakes made by subordinates than would one who supervises closely.

Questions 21-25.

DIRECTIONS: Questions 21 to 25 are to be answered SOLELY on the basis of the information contained in the following paragraph.

Since an organization chart is pictorial in nature, there is a tendency for it to be drawn in an artistically balanced and appealing fashion, regardless of the realities of actual organizational structure. In addition to being subject to this distortion, there is the difficulty of communicating in any organization chart the relative importance or the relative size of various component parts of an organizational structure. Furthermore, because of the need for simplicity of design, an organization chart can never indicate the full extent of the interrelationships among the component parts of an organization. These interrelationships are often just as vital as the specifications which an organization chart endeavors to indicate. Yet, if an organization chart were to be drawn with all the wide variety of criss-crossing communication and cooperation networks existent within a typical organization, the chart would probably be much more confusing than informative. It is also obvious that no organization chart as such can 'prove' or 'disprove' that the organizational structure it represents is effective in realizing the objectives of the organization. At best, an organization chart can only illustrate some of the various factors to be taken into consideration in understanding, devising, or altering organizational arrangements.

21. According to the above paragraph, an organization chart can be expected to portray the   21.____

    A. structure of the organization along somewhat ideal lines
    B. relative size of the organizational units quite accurately
    C. channels of information distribution within the organization graphically
    D. extent of the obligation of each unit to meet the organizational objectives

22. According to the above paragraph, those aspects of internal functioning which are NOT   22.____
shown on an organization chart

    A. can be considered to have little practical application in the operations of the organization
    B. might well be considered to be as important as the structural relationships which a chart does present
    C. could be the cause of considerable confusion in the operation of an organization which is quite large
    D. would be most likely to provide the information needed to determine the overall effectiveness of an organization

23. In the above paragraph, the one of the following conditions which is NOT implied as   23.____
being a defect of an organization chart is that an organization chart may

    A. present a picture of the organizational structure which is different from the structure that actually exists
    B. fail to indicate the comparative size of various organizational units
    C. be limited in its ability to convey some of the meaningful aspects of organizational relationships
    D. become less useful over a period of time during which the organizational facts which it illustrated have changed

24. The one of the following which is the MOST suitable title for the above paragraph is   24.____

    A. The Design and Construction of an Organization Chart
    B. The Informal Aspects of an Organization Chart
    C. The Inherent Deficiencies of an Organization Chart
    D. The Utilization of a Typical Organization Chart

25. It can be INFERRED from the above paragraph that the function of an organization chart   25.____
is to

    A. contribute to the comprehension of the organization form and arrangements
    B. establish the capabilities of the organization to operate effectively
    C. provide a balanced picture of the operations of the organization
    D. eliminate the need for complexity in the organization's structure

KEY (CORRECT ANSWERS)

1.	D		11.	C
2.	C		12.	B
3.	D		13.	B
4.	B		14.	D
5.	A		15.	A
6.	C		16.	A
7.	B		17.	D
8.	A		18.	B
9.	A		19.	B
10.	D		20.	C

21.	A
22.	B
23.	D
24.	C
25.	A

———

TEST 3

DIRECTIONS: Each question or incomplete statement is followed by several suggested answers or completions. Select the one that BEST answers the question or completes the statement. *PRINT THE LETTER OF THE CORRECT ANSWER IN THE SPACE AT THE RIGHT.*

1. Of the following problems that might affect the conduct and outcome of an interview, the MOST troublesome and usually the MOST difficult for the interviewer to control is the

   A. tendency of the interviewee to anticipate the needs and preferences of the inter-viewer
   B. impulse to cut the interviewee off when he seems to have reached the end of an idea
   C. tendency of interviewee attitudes to bias the results
   D. tendency of the interviewer to do most of the talking

   1.____

2. The administrative assistant MOST likely to be a good interviewer is one who

   A. is adept at manipulating people and circumstances toward his objectives
   B. is able to put himself in the position of the interviewee
   C. gets the more difficult questions out of the way at the beginning of the interview
   D. develops one style and technique that can be used in any type of interview

   2.____

3. A good interviewer guards against the tendency to form an overall opinion about an inter-viewee on the basis of a single aspect of the interviewee's make-up.
   This statement refers to a well-known source of error in interviewing known as the

   A. assumption error   B. expectancy error
   C. extension effect   D. halo effect

   3.____

4. In conducting an *exit interview* with an employee who is leaving voluntarily, the inter-viewer's MAIN objective should be to

   A. see that the employee leaves with a good opinion of the organization
   B. learn the true reasons for the employee's resignation
   C. find out if the employee would consider a transfer
   D. try to get the employee to remain on the job

   4.____

5. During an interview, an interviewee unexpectedly discloses a relevant but embarrassing personal fact.
   It would be BEST for the interviewer to

   A. listen calmly, avoiding any gesture or facial expression that would suggest approval or disapproval of what is related
   B. change the subject, since further discussion in this area may reveal other embar-rassing, but irrelevant, personal facts
   C. apologize to the interviewee for having led him to reveal such a fact and promise not to do so again
   D. bring the interview to a close as quickly as possible in order to avoid a discussion which may be distressful to the interviewee

   5.____

6. Suppose that while you are interviewing an applicant for a position in your office, you   6.____
notice a contradiction in facts in two of his responses.
For you to call the contradictions to his attention would be

   A. *inadvisable,* because it reduces the interviewee's level of participation
   B. *advisable,* because getting the facts is essential to a successful interview
   C. *inadvisable,* because the interviewer should use more subtle techniques to resolve
   any discrepancies
   D. *advisable,* because the interviewee should be impressed with the necessity for giv-
   ing consistent answers

7. An interviewer should be aware that an undesirable result of including *leading questions*   7.____
in an interview is to

   A. cause the interviewee to give *yes* or *no* answers with qualification or explanation
   B. encourage the interviewee to discuss irrelevant topics
   C. encourage the interviewee to give more meaningful information
   D. reduce the validity of the information obtained from the interviewee

8. The kind of interview which is PARTICULARLY helpful in getting an employee to tell   8.____
about his complains and grievances is one in which

   A. a pattern has been worked out involving a sequence of exact questions to be
   asked
   B. the interviewee is expected to support his statements with specific evidence
   C. the interviewee is not made to answer specific questions but is encouraged to talk
   freely
   D. the interviewer has specific items on which he wishes to get or give information

9. Suppose you are scheduled to interview a student aide under your supervision concern-   9.____
ing a health problem. You know that some of the questions you will be asking him will
seem embarrassing to him, and that he may resist answering these questions.
In general, to hold these questions for the last part of the interview would be

   A. *desirable;* the intervening time period gives the interviewer an opportunity to plan
   how to ask these sensitive questions
   B. *undesirable;* the student aide will probably feel that he has been tricked when he
   suddenly must answer embarrassing questions
   C. *desirable;* the student aide will probably have increased confidence in the interviewer and be more willing to answer these questions
   D. *undesirable;* questions that are important should not be deferred until the end of
   the interview

10. The House passed an amendment to delete from the omnibus higher education bill a   10.____
section that would have prohibited coeducational colleges and universities from considering sex as a factor in their admissions policy.
According to the above passage, consideration of sex as a factor in the admissions
policy of coeducational colleges and universities would

   A. be permitted by the omnibus higher education bill if passed without further amendment
   B. be prohibited by the amendment to the omnibus higher education bill

C. have been prohibited by the deletion of a section from the omnibus higher education bill
D. have been permitted if the House had failed to pass the amendment

Questions 11-14.

DIRECTIONS: Answer Questions 11 to 14 only according to the information given in the passage below.

The proposition that administrative activity is essentially the same in all organizations appears to underlie some of the practices in the administration of private higher education. Although the practice is unusual in public education, there are numerous instances of industrial, governmental, or military administrators being assigned to private institutions of higher education and, to a lesser extent, of college and university presidents assuming administrative positions in other types of organizations. To test this theory that administrators are interchangeable, there is a need for systematic observation and classification. The myth that an educational administrator must first have experience in the teaching profession is firmly rooted in a long tradition that has historical prestige. The myth is bound up in the expectations of the public and personnel surrounding the administrator. Since administrative success depends significantly on how well an administrator meets the expectations others have of him, the myth may be more powerful than the special experience in helping the administrator attain organizational and educational objectives. Educational administrators who have risen through the teaching profession have often expressed nostalgia for the life of a teacher or scholar, but there is no evidence that this nostalgia contributes to administrative success.

11. Which of the following statements as completed is MOST consistent with the above passage?   11.____
The greatest number of administrators has moved from

   A. industry and the military to government and universities
   B. government and universities to industry and the military
   C. government, the armed forces, and industry to colleges and universities
   D. colleges and universities to government, the armed forces, and industry

12. Of the following, the MOST reasonable inference from the above passage is that a specific area requiring further research is the   12.____

   A. place of myth in the tradition and history of the educational profession
   B. relative effectiveness of educational administrators from inside and outside the teaching profession
   C. performance of administrators in the administration of public colleges
   D. degree of reality behind the nostalgia for scholarly pursuits often expressed by educational administrators

13. According to the above passage, the value to an educational administrator of experience in the teaching profession   13.____

   A. lies in the firsthand knowledge he has acquired of immediate educational problems
   B. may lie in the belief of his colleagues, subordinates, and the public that such experience is necessary

    C.   has been supported by evidence that the experience contributes to administrative success in educational fields

    D.   would be greater if the administrator were able to free himself from nostalgia for his former duties

14.   Of the following, the MOST appropriate title for the above passage is   14.____

    A.   Educational Administration, Its Problems
    B.   The Experience Needed for Educational Administration
    C.   Administration in Higher Education
    D.   Evaluating Administrative Experience

Questions 15-20.

DIRECTIONS: Answer Questions 15 to 20 only according to the information contained in the following paragraph.

Methods of administration of office activities, much of which consists of providing information and 'know-how' needed to coordinate both activities within that particular office and other offices, have been among the last to come under the spotlight of management analysis. Progress has been rapid during the past decade, however, and is now accelerating at such a pace that an 'information revolution' in office management appears to be in the making. Although triggered by technological breakthroughs in electronic computers and other giant steps in mechanization, this information revolution must be attributed to underlying forces, such as the increased complexity of both governmental and private enterprise, and ever-keener competition. Size, diversification, specialization of function, and decentralization are among the forces which make coordination of activities both more imperative and more difficult. Increased competition, both domestic and international, leaves little margin for error in managerial decisions. Several developments during recent years indicate an evolving pattern. In 1960, the American Management Association expanded the scope of its activities and changed the name of its Office Management Division to Administrative Services Division. Also in 1960, the magazine Office Management merged with the magazine American Business, and this new publication was named Administrative Management.

15.   A REASONABLE inference that can be made from the information in the above paragraph is that an important role of the office manager today is to   15.____

    A.   work toward specialization of functions performed by his subordinates
    B.   inform and train subordinates regarding any new developments in computer technology and mechanization
    C.   assist the professional management analysts with the management analysis work in the organization
    D.   supply information that can be used to help coordinate and manage the other activities of the organization

16.   An IMPORTANT reason for the 'information revolution' that has been taking place in office management is the   16.____

    A.   advance made in management analysis in the past decade
    B.   technological breakthrough in electronic computers and mechanization
    C.   more competitive and complicated nature of private business and government
    D.   increased efficiency of office management techniques in the past ten years

17. According to the above paragraph, specialization of function in an organization is MOST   17._____
     likely to result in

     A. the elimination of errors in managerial decisions
     B. greater need to coordinate activities
     C. more competition with other organizations, both domestic and international
     D. a need for office managers with greater flexibility

18. The word *evolving,* as used in the third from last sentence in the above paragraph,   18._____
     means *most nearly*

     A. developing by gradual changes
     B. passing on to others
     C. occurring periodically
     D. breaking up into separate, constituent parts

19. Of the following, the MOST reasonable implication of the changes in names mentioned in   19._____
     the last part of the above paragraph is that these groups are attempting to

     A. professionalize the field of office management and the title of Office Manager
     B. combine two publications into one because of the increased costs of labor and
         materials
     C. adjust to the fact that the field of office management is broadening
     D. appeal to the top managerial people rather than the office management people in
         business and government

20. According to the above paragraph, intense competition among domestic and interna-   20._____
     tional enterprises makes it MOST important for an organization's managerial staff to

     A. coordinate and administer office activities with other activities in the organization
     B. make as few errors in decision-making as possible
     C. concentrate on decentralization and reduction of size of the individual divisions of
         the organization
     D. restrict decision-making only to top management officials

_____

KEY (CORRECT ANSWERS)

1.	A	11.	C
2.	B	12.	B
3.	D	13.	B
4.	B	14.	B
5.	A	15.	D
6.	B	16.	C
7.	D	17.	B
8.	C	18.	A
9.	C	19.	C
10.	A	20.	B

———

EXAMINATION SECTION
TEST 1

DIRECTIONS: Each question or incomplete statement is followed by several suggested answers or completions. Select the one that BEST answers the question or completes the statement. *PRINT THE LETTER OF THE CORRECT ANSWER IN THE SPACE AT THE RIGHT.*

1. In discussing with a subordinate the assignment which you are giving him, it is MOST important that you place greatest stress on

    A. the immediate job to be done
    B. what was accomplished in the past
    C. the long-term goals of the organization
    D. what others have accomplished

1.____

2. Personal friendship and intimacy exhibited by the administrative assistant toward his subordinates should ALWAYS be

    A. kept to a bare minimum
    B. free and unrestricted
    C. in accordance with the personal qualities of each individual subordinate
    D. tempered by the need for objectivity

2.____

3. Assume that one of the office assistants under your supervision approaches you and asks if you would give her advice on some problems that she is having with her husband. Of the following, the MOST appropriate action for you to take is to

    A. tell her that she would be making a mistake in discussing it with you
    B. listen briefly to her problem and then suggest how she might get help in solving it
    C. give her whatever advice she needs based on your knowledge or experience in this area
    D. refer her to a lawyer specializing in marital problems

3.____

4. When you return from lunch one day, you find Miss P, one of your subordinates, in your office crying uncontrollably. When she calms down, she tells you that Mr. T, another subordinate, insulted her but she would prefer not to give details because they are very personal.
Your IMMEDIATE reaction should be to

    A. reprimand Mr. T for his callousness
    B. reprimand the worker in your office for not controlling herself
    C. get as much information as possible about exactly what happened
    D. tell Miss P that she will have to take care of her own affairs

4.____

5. If one of the office assistants under your supervision does not seem to be able to get along well with the other employees, the FIRST step that you should take in such a situation should be to try to find out

    A. more about the background of the office assistant
    B. the reason the office assistant has difficulty in getting along
    C. if another department would be interested in employing the office assistant
    D. the procedures required for dismissal of the office assistant

5.____

6. Suppose that you expect that your department will send two of your subordinates for out-   6.____
side training on the use of new office equipment while others will be trained on the job.
When preparing a yearly budget and schedule for the personnel that you supervise,
training costs to be paid for by the department should be

    A. excluded and treated separately as a special request when the specific training
need arises
    B. estimated and included in the budget and manpower schedules
    C. left out of the schedule since personnel are thoroughly trained before assignment
to a position
    D. considered only if training involves time away from the job

7. There is a rumor going around your department that one of the administrative assistants   7.____
is going to resign.
Since it is not true, the BEST action to take would be to

    A. find the person starting the rumor, and advise him that disciplinary action will follow
if the rumors do not stop
    B. disregard the rumor since the grapevine is always inaccurate
    C. tell the truth about the situation to those concerned
    D. start another rumor yourself that contradicts this rumor

8. Suppose a student is concerned over the possibility of failing a course and losing matric-   8.____
ulated status. He comes to you for advice.
The BEST thing for you to do is to

    A. tell the student it is not your function to discuss student problems
    B. impress the student with the importance of academic performance and suggest
that more study is necessary
    C. send the student to a career counselor for testing
    D. suggest that he see the instructor or appropriate faculty advisor depending on the
cause of the problem

9. A member of the faculty had requested that an overhead projector be reserved for a   9.____
seminar. At the time of the seminar, the projector has not been placed in the room, and
you find that one of your office assistants forgot to send the request to the building staff.
Of the following possible actions, which one should be taken FIRST?

    A. See to it that the projector is moved to the seminar room immediately.
    B. Personally reprimand the subordinate responsible.
    C. Suggest rescheduling the seminar.
    D. Tell the faculty member that the problem was caused by a fault in the machine.

10. Assume that you have to give work assignments to a male office assistant and a female   10.____
office assistant. It would be BEST to

    A. allow the woman to have first choice of assignments
    B. give the female preference in assignments requiring patience
    C. give the male preference in assignments requiring physical action
    D. make assignments to each on the basis of demonstrated ability and interest

11. In the *initial* phase of training a new employee to perform his job, which of the following approaches is MOST desirable?

    A. Have him read the office manual
    B. Tell him to watch the other employees
    C. Give him simple tasks to perform
    D. Have him do exactly what everyone else is doing

11.____

12. Assume that one of the employees under your supervision performs her work adequately, but you feel that she might be more productive if she changed some of her methods.
You should

    A. discuss with her those changes which you think would be helpful
    B. refrain from saying anything since her work is adequate
    C. suggest that she might be helped by talking to a guidance counselor
    D. assign her to another job

12.____

13. One of the office assistants under your supervision complains to you that the report which you assigned her to prepare is monotonous work and unnecessary. The report is a monthly compilation of figures which you submit to your superior.
Of the following, the *best* action to take FIRST is to

    A. ask her why she feels the work is unnecessary
    B. tell her that she is employed to do whatever work is assigned to her
    C. have her do other work at the same time to provide more interest
    D. assign the report to another subordinate

13.____

14. Of the following, the GREATEST advantage of keeping records of the quantity of work produced by the office assistants under your supervision is to

    A. have the statistics available in case they are required
    B. enable you to take appropriate action in case of increase, decrease, or other variation in output
    C. provide a basis for promotion or other personnel action
    D. give you a basis for requesting additional employees

14.____

15. It is not possible to achieve maximum productivity from your subordinates *unless* they are told

    A. what the rewards are for their performance
    B. how they will be punished for failure
    C. what it is they are expected to do
    D. that they must work hard if they are to succeed

15.____

16. Suppose that you observe that one of the assistants on your staff is involved with an extremely belligerent student who is demanding information that is not readily available in your department. One staff member is becoming visibly upset and is apparently about to lose his temper.
Under these circumstances, it would be BEST for you to

16.____

A. leave the room and let the situation work itself out
B. let the assistant lose his temper, then intervene and calm both parties at the same time
C. step in immediately and try to calm the student in order to suggest more expedient ways of getting the information
D. tell the student to come back and discuss the situation when he can do it calmly

17. Suppose you have explained an assignment to a newly appointed clerk and the clerk has demonstrated her ability to do the work. After a short period of time, the clerk tells you that she is afraid of incorrectly completing the assignment.
Of the following, the BEST course of action for you to take is to   17.____

A. tell her to observe another clerk who is doing the same type of work
B. explain to her the importance of the assignment and tell her not to be nervous
C. assign her another task which is easier to perform
D. try to allay her fears and encourage her to try to do the work

Questions 18-22.

DIRECTIONS: Questions 18 through 22 consist of the names of students who have applied for a certain college program and are to be classified according to the criteria described below.

The following table gives pertinent data for 6 different applicants with regard to:
Grade averages, which are expressed on a scale running from
        0 (low) to 4 (high);
Scores on qualifying test, which run from 200 (low) to 800 (high); Related work experience, which is expressed in number of months; Personal references, which are rated from 1 (low) to 5 (high).

Applicant	Grade Average	Test Score	Work Experience	Reference
Jones	2.2	620	24	3
Perez	3.5	650	0	5
Lowitz	3.2	420	2	4
Uncker	2.1	710	15	2
Farrow	2.8	560	0	3
Shapiro	3.0	560	12	4

An administrative assistant is in charge of the initial screening process for the program. This process requires classifying applicants into the following four groups:

A. SUPERIOR CANDIDATES. Unless the personal reference rating is lower than 3, all applicants with grade averages of 3.0 or higher and test scores of 600 or higher are classified as superior candidates.
B. GOOD CANDIDATES. Unless the personal reference rating is lower than 3, all applicants with one of the following combinations of grade averages and test scores are classified as good candidates: (1) grade average of 2.5 to 2.9 and test score of 600 or higher; (2) grade average of 3.0 or higher and test score of 550 to 599.
C. POSSIBLE CANDIDATES. Applicants with one of the following combinations of qualifications are classified as possible candidates: (1) grade average of 2.5 to 2.9 and test score of 550 to 599 and a personal reference rating of 3 or higher; (2) grade average of 2.0 to 2.4 and test score of 500 or higher and at least 21 months' work experience and a personal reference rating of 3 or higher; (3) a combination

of grade average and test score that would otherwise qualify as *superior* or *good* but a personal reference score lower than 3.

D. REJECTED CANDIDATES. Applicants who do not fall in any of the above groups are to be rejected.

EXAMPLE

Jones' grade average of 2.2 does not meet the standard for either a superior candidate (grade average must be 3.0 or higher) or a good candidate (grade average must be 2.5 to 2.9). Grade average of 2.2 does not qualify Jones as a possible candidate if Jones has a test score of 500 or higher, at least 21 months' work experience, and a personal reference rating of 3 or higher. Since Jones has a test score of 620, 24 months' work experience, and a reference rating of 3, Jones is a possible candidate. The answer is C.

Answer Questions 18 through 22 as explained above, indicating for each whether the applicant should be classified as a

A.	superior candidate	B.	good candidate
C.	possible candidate	D.	rejected candidate

18. Perez   18._____

19. Lowitz   19._____

20. Uncker   20._____

21. Farrow   21._____

22. Shapiro   22._____

23. A new training program is being set up for which certain new forms will be needed. You   23._____
have been asked to design these forms.
Of the following, the FIRST step you should take in planning the forms is

    A. finding out the exact purpose for which each form will be used
    B. deciding what size of paper should be used for each form
    C. determining whether multiple copies will be needed for any of the forms
    D. setting up a new filing system to handle the new forms

24. You have been asked to write a report on methods of hiring and training new employees.   24._____
Your report is going to be about ten pages long.
For the convenience of your readers, a brief summary of your findings should

    A. appear at the beginning of your report
    B. be appended to the report as a postscript
    C. be circulated in a separate memo
    D. be inserted in tabular form in the middle of your report

25. Assume that your department is being moved to new and larger quarters, and that you   25._____
have been asked to suggest an office layout for the central clerical office. Of the following, your FIRST step in planning the new layout should ordinarily be to

    A. find out how much money has been budgeted for furniture and equipment
    B. make out work-flow and traffic-flow charts for the clerical operations
    C. measure each piece of furniture and equipment that is presently in use
    D. determine which files should be moved to a storage area or destroyed

KEY (CORRECT ANSWERS)

1.	A		11.	C
2.	D		12.	A
3.	B		13.	A
4.	C		14.	B
5.	B		15.	C
6.	B		16.	C
7.	C		17.	D
8.	D		18.	A
9.	A		19.	D
10.	D		20.	D

21.	C
22.	B
23.	A
24.	A
25.	B

———

TEST 2

DIRECTIONS: Each question or incomplete statement is followed by several suggested answers or completions. Select the one that BEST answers the question or completes the statement. *PRINT THE LETTER OF THE CORRECT ANSWER IN THE SPACE AT THE RIGHT.*

1. In modern office layouts, screens and dividers are often used instead of walls to set off working groups. Advantages given for this approach have included all of the following EXCEPT   1.____

    A. more frequent communication between different working groups
    B. reduction in general noise level
    C. fewer objections from employees who are transferred to different groups
    D. cost savings from increased sharing of office equipment

2. Of the following, the CHIEF reason for moving less active material from active to inactive files is to   2.____

    A. dispose of material that no longer has any use
    B. keep the active files down to a manageable size
    C. make sure that no material over a year old remains in active files
    D. separate temporary records from permanent records

3. The use of a microfiche system for information storage and retrieval would make MOST sense in an office where   3.____

    A. a great number of documents must be kept available for permanent reference
    B. documents are ordinarily kept on file for less than six months
    C. filing is a minor and unimportant part of office work
    D. most of the records on file are working forms on which additional entries are frequently made

4. The work loads in different offices fluctuate greatly over the course of a year. Ordinarily, the MOST economical way of handling a peak load in a specific office is to   4.____

    A. hire temporary help from an outside agency
    B. require regular employees to put in overtime
    C. use employees from other offices that are not busy
    D. buy special equipment for operations that can be automated

5. A faculty member has given you a long list of student grades to be typed. Since your typed list will be the basis for permanent records, it is essential that it contain no errors. The BEST way of checking this typed list is to   5.____

    A. ask the faculty member to glance over the typed version and have him correct any mistakes
    B. have someone read the handwritten list aloud, while you check the typed list as each item is read
    C. read the typed list yourself to see that it makes good sense and that there are no omissions or duplications
    D. make a spot-check by comparing several entries in the typed list against the original entries on the handwritten list

6. It is necessary to purchase a machine for your department which will be used to make single copies of documents and to make copies of memos that are distributed to as many as 150 people.
   Of the following kinds of machines, which one is BEST suited for your department's purposes?
   A(n)

   A. laser copier
   C. inkjet printer
   B. fax machine
   D. multipage scanner

   6.____

7. Suppose that faculty members have fallen into the habit of asking clerical employees in your department to perform messenger service between your building and other parts of the school. Such demands are becoming increasingly common, and you feel that the two or three man-hours per day involved is too much. Furthermore, these assignments disrupt the work of the department.
   Of the following solutions, which one is most likely to result in the GREATEST efficiency?

   A. Hire a full-time messenger whose only job will be to run intra-school errands
   B. Establish a rule that no employees in your department will act as messengers under any circumstances, and that all materials must be sent by ordinary interoffice mail
   C. Notify other departments that from now on they must use their own employees for messenger service to or from your building
   D. Allow the clerical employees to perform messenger service only in cases of urgent need, and have interoffice mail used in all other cases

   7.____

8. A new employee is trying to file records for three different students whose names are Robinson, John L., Robinson, John, and Robinson, John Leonard. The employee does not know in what order the records should be filed.
   You should

   A. tell the employee to use whatever order seems most convenient
   B. suggest that all the records be put in one folder and arranged chronologically according to date of enrollment
   C. explain that, by the *nothing-before-something* principle, John comes first, John L. second, and John Leonard last
   D. instruct the employee to keep them together but arrange them chronologically according to date of birth

   8.____

9. An *out card* or *out guide* should be placed in a file drawer to mark the location of material that

   A. has not yet been received
   B. should be transferred to an inactive file
   C. has been temporarily removed
   D. is no longer needed

   9.____

10. Assume that your office does not presently have a formal records-retention program. Your supervisor has suggested that such a program be set up, and has asked you to make a study and submit your recommendations.
    The FIRST step in your study should be to

    10.____

    A.   find out how long it has been since the files were last cleaned out
    B.   take an inventory of the types of materials now in the files
    C.   learn how much storage space you can obtain for old records
    D.   decide which files should be thrown out instead of being stored

11.   In an organization where a great deal of time and money is spent on information man-   11._____
        agement, it often makes sense to use a *systems analysis* approach in reviewing opera-
        tions and deciding how they can be carried out more efficiently.
        Of the following, the FIRST question that a *systems analysis* should ask about any
        procedure is

    A.   whether the procedure can be handled by automatic data-processing equipment
    B.   exactly how the procedure is meshed with other existing procedures used in the
        organization
    C.   how many employees should be hired to carry out the present procedure
    D.   what is the end result that the use of the procedure is supposed to achieve

12.   You have been notified that a *work simplification* study is going to be carried out in your   12._____
        department.
        The one of the following which is MOST likely to be the purpose of this study is to

    A.   increase the productivity of the office by eliminating unnecessary procedures and
        irrelevant record keeping
    B.   produce a new office manual that explains current procedures in a simple and eas-
        ily understandable way
    C.   determine whether there are any procedures so simple that they can be handled
        by untrained workers
    D.   substitute computer processing for all operations that are now performed manually

13.   Suppose that a cost study has been made of various clerical procedures carried out in   13._____
        your college, and that the study shows that the average cost of a dictated business letter
        is over $5.00 per letter.
        Of the following cost factors that go into making up this total cost, the LARGEST *single*
        factor is certain to be the cost of

    A.   stationery and postage   B.   office machinery
    C.   labor   D.   office rental

14.   Which of the following software programs is BEST for collecting and sorting data,   14._____
        creating graphs and preparing spreadsheets?

    A.   Microsoft Excel   B.   Microsoft Word
    C.   Microsoft Powerpoint   D.   QuarkXPress

15.   Which of the following software programs is BEST for creating visual presentations   15._____
        containing text, photos and charts?

    A.   Microsoft Excel   B.   Microsoft Outlook
    C.   Microsoft Powerpoint   D.   Adobe Photoshop

16. A supervisor asks you to e-mail a file that has been saved on your computer as a photograph. Since you do not remember the file name, you must search by file type. Which of the following file extensions should you run a search for?

   A. .html   B. .pdf   C. .jpg   D. .doc

16._____

17. In records management, the term *vital records* refers generally to papers that

   A. are essential to life
   B. are needed for an office to continue operating after fire or other disaster
   C. contain statistics about birth and death
   D. can be easily replaced

17._____

18. A city agency maintains a complete set of records on its clients on a central computer. A branch office finds that it frequently needs access to this data.
A computer output device which could be installed in the branch office to provide the data is called a

   A. sorter   B. tabulator
   C. card punch   D. terminal

18._____

19. A certain employee is paid at the rate of $9.10 per hour, with time-and-a-half for overtime. Hours in excess of 40 hours a week count as overtime. During the past week the employee put in 44 working hours.
The employee's gross wages for the week are MOST NEARLY

   A. $368   B. $396   C. $414   D. $444

19._____

20. You are making a report on the number of inside and outside calls handled by a particular switchboard. Over a 5-day period, the total number of all inside and outside calls handled by the switchboard was 2,314. The average number of inside calls per day was 274. You cannot find one day's tally of outside calls, but the total number of outside calls for the other four days was 776.
Fron this information, how many outside calls must have been reported on the missing tally?

   A. 168   B. 190   C. 194   D. 274

20._____

21. One typist can type 100 address labels in 1 hour. Another typist can type 100 address labels in 1 hour and 15 minutes. If there are 450 address labels to be typed and both typists are put to work on the job, how soon can they be expected to finish the work?
In _____ hours.

   A. $2\frac{1}{4}$ B. $2\frac{1}{2}$ C. $4\frac{1}{2}$ D. 5

21._____

22. A floor plan has been prepared for a new building, drawn to a scale of $\frac{1}{2}$ inch = 1 foot. A certain area is drawn 1 foot long and $7\frac{1}{2}$ inches wide on the floor plan.

    The actual dimensions of this area in the new building are _____ feet long and _____ feet wide.

    A.   6; $3\frac{1}{4}$ B.   12; $7\frac{1}{2}$ C.   20; 15   D.   24; 15

22._____

23. In recent years a certain college has admitted a number of students with high school grades of C-plus or lower. It has usually turned out that an average of *65%* of these students completed their freshman year. Last year 340 such students were admitted. By the end of the year, 102 of these students were no longer in college, but the others completed successfully.
    How many MORE students completed the year than would have been expected, based on the average results of previous years?

    A.   14   B.   17   C.   39   D.   119

23._____

24. The morale of employees is an important factor in the maintenance of job interest. Which of the following is generally LEAST valuable in strengthening morale?

    A.   Attempting to take a personal interest in one's subordinates
    B.   Encouraging employees to speak openly about their opinions and suggestions
    C.   Fostering a feeling of group spirit among the workers
    D.   Having all employees work at the same rate

24._____

25. Of the following, the BEST way for a supervisor to determine when *further* on-the-job training in a particular work area is needed is by

    A.   asking the employees
    B.   evaluating the employees' work performance
    C.   determining the ratio of idle time to total work time
    D.   classifying the jobs in the work area

25._____

_____

KEY (CORRECT ANSWERS)

1.	B		11.	D
2.	B		12.	A
3.	A		13.	C
4.	C		14.	A
5.	B		15.	C
6.	A		16.	C
7.	D		17.	B
8.	C		18.	D
9.	C		19.	C
10.	B		20.	A

21.	B
22.	D
23.	B
24.	D
25.	B

———

EXAMINATION SECTION
TEST 1

DIRECTIONS: Each question or incomplete statement is followed by several suggested answers or completions. Select the one that BEST answers the question or completes the statement. *PRINT THE LETTER OF THE CORRECT ANSWER IN THE SPACE AT THE RIGHT.*

Questions 1-6.

DIRECTIONS: Questions 1 through 6 each consist of four sentences. Choose the one sentence in each set of four that would be BEST for a formal letter or report. Consider grammar and appropriate usage.

1.   A.   These statements can be depended on, for their truth has been guaranteed by reliable city employees.
     B.   Reliable city employees guarantee the facts with regards to the truth of these statements.
     C.   Most all these statements have been supported by city employees who are reliable and can be depended upon.
     D.   The city employees which have guaranteed these statements are reliable.

1.____

2.   A.   I believe the letter was addressed to either my associate or I.
     B.   If properly addressed, the letter will reach my associate and I.
     C.   My associate's name, as well as mine, was on the letter.
     D.   The letter had been addressed to myself and my associate.

2.____

3.   A.   The secretary would have corrected the errors if she knew that the supervisor would see the report.
     B.   The supervisor reprimanded the secretary, whom she believed had made careless errors.
     C.   Many errors were found in the report which she typed and could not disregard them.
     D.   The errors in the typed report were so numerous that they could hardly be overlooked.

3.____

4.   A.   His consultant was as pleased as he with the success of the project.
     B.   The success of the project pleased both his consultant and he.
     C.   he and also his consultant was pleased with the success of the project.
     D.   Both his consultant and he was pleased with the success of the project.

4.____

5.   A.   Since the letter did not contain the needed information, it was not real useful to him.
     B.   Being that the letter lacked the needed information, he could not use it.
     C.   Since the letter lacked the needed information, it was of no use to him.
     D.   This letter was useless to him because there was no needed information in it.

5.____

6.　A.　Scarcely had the real estate tax increase been declared than the notices were　　6.＿＿＿
　　　　sent out.
　　B.　They had no sooner declared the real estate tax increases when they sent the
　　　　notices to the owners.
　　C.　The city had hardly declared the real estate tax increase till the notices were pre-
　　　　pared for mailing.
　　D.　No sooner had the real estate tax increase been declared than the notices were
　　　　sent out.

Questions 7-14.

DIRECTIONS:　Answer Questions 7 through 14 on the basis of the following passage.

　　　Important figures in education and in public affairs have recommended development of a
private organization sponsored in part by various private foundations which would offer
installment payment plans to full-time matriculated students in accredited colleges and universities in the United States and Canada. Contracts would be drawn to cover either tuition
and fees, or tuition, fees, room and board in college facilities, from one year up to and including six years. A special charge, which would vary with the length of the contract, would be
added to the gross repayable amount. This would be in addition to interest at a rate which
would vary with the income of the parents. There would be a 3% annual interest charge for
families with total income, before income taxes of $10,000 or less. The rate would increase by
1/10 of 1% for every $200 of additional net income in excess of $10,000 up to a maximum of
10% interest. Contracts would carry an insurance provision on the life of the parent or guardian who signs the contract; all contracts must have the signature of a parent or guardian. Payment would be scheduled in equal monthly installments.

7.　Which of the following students would be eligible for the payment plan described in the　　7.＿＿＿
　　above passage?
　　A

　　A.　matriculated student taking 6 semester hours toward a graduate degree at CCNY
　　B.　matriculated student taking 17 semester hours toward an undergraduate degree at
　　　　Brooklyn College
　　C.　CCNY graduate matriculated at the University of Mexico, taking 18 semester hours
　　　　toward a graduate degree
　　D.　student taking 18 semester hours in a special pre-matriculation program at Hunter
　　　　College

8.　According to the above passage, the organization described would be sponsored in part　　8.＿＿＿
　　by

　　A.　private foundations
　　B.　colleges and universities
　　C.　persons in the field of education
　　D.　persons in public life

9.　Which of the following expenses could NOT be covered by a contract with the organiza-　　9.＿＿＿
　　tion described in the above passage?

　　A.　Tuition amounting to $4,000 per year
　　B.　Registration and laboratory fees

C.   Meals at restaurants near the college
D.   Rent for an apartment in a college dormitory

10.   The total amount to be paid would include ONLY the   10._____

A.   principal
B.   principal and interest
C.   principal, interest, and special charge
D.   principal, interest, special charge, and fee

11.   The contract would carry insurance on the   11._____

A.   life of the student
B.   life of the student's parents
C.   income of the parents of the student
D.   life of the parent who signed the contract

12.   The interest rate for an annual loan of $5,000 from the organization described in the pas-   12._____
      sage for a student whose family's net income was $11,000 should be

A.   3%   B.   3.5%   C.   4%   D.   4.5%

13.   The interest rate for an annual loan of $7,000 from the organization described in the pas-   13._____
      sage for a student whose family's net income was $20,000 should be

A.   5%   B.   8%   C.   9%   D.   10%

14.   John Lee has submitted an application for the installment payment plan described in the   14._____
      passage. John's mother and father have a store which grossed $100,000 last year, but
      the income which the family received from the store was $18,000 before taxes. They also
      had $1,000 income from stock dividends. They paid $2,000 in income taxes.
      The amount of income upon which the interest should be based is

A. $17,000   B. $18,000   C. $19,000   D. $21,000

15.   One of the MOST important techniques for conducting good interviews is   15._____

A.   asking the applicant questions in rapid succession, thereby keeping the conversa-
     tion properly focused
B.   listening carefully to all that the applicant has to say, making mental notes of possi-
     ble areas for follow-up
C.   indicating to the applicant the criteria and standards on which you will base your
     judgment
D.   making sure that you are interrupted above five minutes before you wish to end so
     that you can keep on schedule

16.   You are planning to conduct preliminary interviews of applicants for an important position   16._____
      in your department. Which of the following planning considerations is LEAST likely to
      contribute to successful interviews?

A.   Make provisions to conduct interviews in privacy
B.   Schedule your appointments so that interviews will be short
C.   Prepare a list of your objectives
D.   Learn as much as you can about the applicant before the interview.

17. In interviewing job applicants, which of the following usually does NOT have to be done before the end of the interview?   17.____

    A. Making a decision to hire an applicant
    B. Securing information from applicants
    C. Giving information to applicants
    D. Establishing a friendly relationship with applicants

18. In the process of interviewing applicants for a position on your staff, the one of the following which would be BEST is to   18.____

    A. make sure all applicants are introduced to the other members of your staff prior to the formal interview
    B. make sure the applicant does not ask questions about the job or the department
    C. avoid having the applicant talk with the staff under any circumstances
    D. introduce applicants to some of the staff at the conclusion of a successful interview

19. While interviewing a job applicant, you ask why the applicant left his last job. The applicant does not answer immediately.   19.____
Of the following, the BEST action to take at that point is to

    A. wait until he answers
    B. ask another question
    C. repeat the question in a loud voice
    D. ask him why he does not answer

20. Which of the following actions would be LEAST desirable for you to take when you have to conduct an interview?   20.____

    A. Set a relaxed and friendly atmosphere
    B. Plan your interview ahead of time
    C. Allow the person interviewed to structure the interview as he wishes
    D. Include some stock or standard question which you ask everyone

21. You know that a student applying for a job in your office has done well in college except for two courses in science. However, when you ask him about his grades, his reply is vague and general.   21.____
It would be BEST for you to

    A. lead the applicant to admitting doing poorly in science to be sure that the facts are correct
    B. judge the applicant's tact and skill in handling what may be for him a personally sensitive question
    C. immediately confront the applicant with the facts and ask for an explanation
    D. ignore the applicant's response since you have the transcript

22. A college student has applied for a position with your department. Prior to conducting an interview of the job applicant, it would be LEAST helpful for you to have   22.____

    A. a personal resume   B. a job description
    C. references   D. hiring requirements

23. Job applicants tend to be nervous during interviews. Which of the following techniques is MOST likely to put such an applicant at ease?

    23.____

    A. Try to establish rapport by asking general questions which are easily answered by the applicant
    B. Ask the applicant to describe his career objectives immediately, thus minimizing the anxiety caused by waiting
    C. Start the interview with another member of the staff present so that the applicant does not feel alone
    D. Proceed as rapidly as possible, since the emotional state of the applicant is none of your concern

24. Of the following abilities, the one which is LEAST important in conducting an interview is the ability to

    24.____

    A. ask the interviewee pertinent questions
    B. evaluate the interviewee on the basis of appearance
    C. evaluate the responses of the interviewee
    D. gain the cooperation of the interviewee

25. One of the techniques of management often used by supervisors is performance appraisal.
Which of the following is NOT one of the objectives of performance appraisal?

    25.____

    A. Improve staff performance
    B. Determine individual training needs
    C. Improve organizational structure
    D. Set standards and performance criteria for employees

———

KEY (CORRECT ANSWERS)

1.	A	11.	D
2.	C	12.	B
3.	D	13.	B
4.	A	14.	C
5.	C	15.	B
6.	D	16.	B
7.	B	17.	A
8.	A	18.	D
9.	C	19.	A
10.	C	20.	C

21.	B
22.	C
23.	A
24.	B
25.	C

———

TEST 2

1. Examine the following sentence, and then choose the BEST statement about it from the choices below.
Clerks are expected to receive visitors, to answer telephones, and miscellaneous clerical work must be done.

    A. This sentence is an example of effective writing.
    B. This is a *run-on* sentence.
    C. The three ideas in this sentence are not parallel, and therefore they should be divided into separate sentences.
    D. The three ideas in this sentence are parallel, but they are not expressed in parallel form.

1.____

2. Examine the following sentence, and then choose from below the word which should be inserted in the blank space.
Mr. Luce is a top-notch interviewer, _____ he is very reliable.

    A. but   B. and   C. however   D. for

2.____

3. Examine the following sentence, and then choose from below the words which should be inserted in the blank spaces.
The committee _____ sent in _____ report.

    A. has; it's   B. has; their
    C. have; its   D. has; its

3.____

4. Examine the following sentence, and then choose from below the words which should be inserted in the blank spaces.
An organization usually contains more than just a few people; usually the membership is _____ enough so that close personal relationships among _____ impossible.

    A. large; are   B. large; found
    C. small; becomes   D. small; is

4.____

5. Of the following, the BEST reference book to use to find a synonym for a common word is a(n)

    A. thesaurus   B. dictionary
    C. encyclopedia   D. catalog

5.____

Questions 6-10.

DIRECTIONS: Questions 6 through 10 concern college students who have just completed their junior year for whom you must calculate grade averages for the year. These averages are to be based on the following table showing the number of credit hours for each student during the year at each of the grade levels: A, B, C, D, and F. How these letter grades may be translated into numerical grades is indicated in the first column of the table.

Grade Value	Credit Hours- Junior Year					
	King	Lewis	Martin	Nonkin	Ottly	Perry
A = 95	12	6	15	3	9	-
B = 85	9	15	6	12	9	3
C = 75	6	9	9	12	3	27
D = 65	3	-	3	3	6	-
F = 0	-	-	-	3	-	-

Calculating a grade average for an individual student is a 4-step process:

I. Multiply each grade value by the number of credit hours for which the student received that grade
II. Add these multiplication products for each student
III. Add the student's total credit hours
IV. Divide the multiplication product total by the total number of credit hours
V. Round the result, if there is a decimal place, to the nearest whole number. A number ending in .5 would be rounded to the next higher number

Example

Using student King's grades as an example, his grade average can be calculated by going through the following four steps:

I.
$$95 \times 12 = 1140$$
$$85 \times 9 = 765$$
$$75 \times 6 = 450$$
$$65 \times 3 = 195$$
$$0 \times 0 = 0$$

III.
12
9
6
3
0
30 TOTAL credit hours

II. Total = 2550

IV. Divide 2550 by 30: $\frac{2550}{30} = 85$

King's grade average is 85.

Answer Questions 6 through 10 on the basis of the information given above.

6. The grade average of Lewis is

A. 83   B. 84   C. 85   D. 86

7. The grade average of Martin is

A. 83   B. 84   C. 85   D. 86

8. The grade average of Nonkin is

A. 72   B. 73   C. 79   D. 80

9. Student Ottly must attain a grade average of 85 in each of his years in college to be accepted into graduate school.
If, in summer school during his junior year, he takes two 3-credit courses and receives a grade of 85 in one and 95 in the other, his grade average for his junior year will then be MOST NEARLY

A. 82   B. 83   C. 84   D. 85

6._____

7._____

8._____

9._____

10. If Perry takes an additional 3-credit course during the year and receives a grade of 95,   10._____
his grade average will be increased to approximately

    A. 74   B. 76   C. 78   D. 80

11. You are in charge of verifying employees' qualifications. This involves telephoning previ-   11._____
ous employers and schools. One of the applications which you are reviewing contains
information which you are almost certain is correct on the basis of what the employee
has told you.
The BEST thing to do is to

    A. check the information again with the employee
    B. perform the required verification procedures
    C. accept the information as valid
    D. ask a superior to verify the information

12. The practice of immediately identifying oneself and one's place of employment when   12._____
contacting persons on the telephone is

    A. *good,* because the receiver of the call can quickly identify the caller and establish a
        frame of reference
    B. *good,* because it helps to set the caller at ease with the other party
    C. *poor,* because it is not necessary to divulge that information when making general
        calls
    D. *poor,* because it takes longer to arrive at the topic to be discussed

13. A supervisor, Miss Smith, meets with a group of subordinates and tells them how they   13._____
should perform certain tasks. The meeting is highly successful. She then attends a meeting to discuss common problems with a group of fellow supervisors with duties similar to
her own. When she tells them how their subordinates should perform the same tasks,
some of the other supervisors become angry.
Of the following, the MOST likely reason for this anger is that

    A. tension is to be expected in situations in which supervisors deal with each other
    B. the other supervisors are jealous of Miss Smith's knowledge
    C. Miss Smith should not tell other supervisors what methods she uses
    D. Miss Smith does not correctly perceive her role in relation to other supervisors

14. There is considerable rivalry among employees in a certain department over location of   14._____
desks. It is the practice of the supervisor to assign desks without any predetermined
plan. The supervisor is reconsidering his procedure.
In assigning desks, PRIMARY consideration should ordinarily be given to

    A. past practices
    B. flow of work
    C. employee seniority
    D. social relations among employees

15. Assume that, when you tell some of the typists under your supervision that the letters they prepare have too many errors, they contend that the letters are readable and that they obtain more satisfaction from their jobs if they do not have to be as concerned about errors.
These typists are

    A. *correct,* because the ultimate objective should be job satisfaction
    B. *incorrect,* because every job should be performed perfectly
    C. *correct,* because they do not compose the letters themselves
    D. *incorrect,* because their satisfaction is not the only consideration

15._____

16. Which of the following possible conditions is LEAST likely to represent a hindrance to effective communication?

    A. The importance of a situation may not be apparent.
    B. Words may mean different things to different people.
    C. The recipient of a communication may respond to it, sometimes unfavorably.
    D. Communications may affect the self-interest of those communicating.

16._____

17. You are revising the way in which your unit handles records.
One of the BEST ways to make sure that the change will be implemented with a minimum of difficulty is to

    A. allow everyone on the staff who is affected by the change to have an opportunity to contribute their ideas to the new procedures
    B. advise only the key members of your staff in advance so that they can help you enforce the new method when it is implemented
    C. give the assignment of implementation to the newest member of the unit
    D. issue a memorandum announcing the change and stating that complaints will not be tolerated

17._____

18. One of your assistants is quite obviously having personal problems that are affecting his work performance.
As a supervisor, it would be MOST appropriate for you to

    A. avoid any inquiry into the nature of the situation since this is not one of your responsibilities
    B. avoid any discussion of personal problems on the basis that there is nothing you could do about them anyhow
    C. help the employee obtain appropriate help with these problems
    D. advise the employee that personal problems cannot be considered when evaluating work performance

18._____

19. The key to improving communication with your staff and other departments is the development of an awareness of the importance of communication.
Which of the following is NOT a good suggestion for developing this awareness?

    A. Be willing to look at your own attitude toward how you communicate.
    B. Be sensitive and receptive to reactions to what you tell people.
    C. Make sure all communication is in writing.
    D. When giving your subordinates directions, try to put yourself in their place and see if your instructions still make sense.

19._____

20. One of the assistants on your staff has neglected to complete an important assignment   20._____
on schedule. You feel that a reprimand is necessary.
When speaking to the employee, it would usually be LEAST desirable to

   A. display your anger to show the employee how strongly you feel about the problem
   B. ask several questions about the reasons for failure to complete the assignment
   C. take the employee aside so that nobody else is present when you discuss the matter
   D. give the employee as much time as he needs to explain exactly what happened

---

KEY (CORRECT ANSWERS)

1.	D	11.	B
2.	B	12.	A
3.	D	13.	D
4.	A	14.	B
5.	A	15.	D
6.	B	16.	C
7.	C	17.	A
8.	B	18.	C
9.	C	19.	C
10.	C	20.	A

EXAMINATION SECTION
TEST 1

DIRECTIONS: Each question or incomplete statement is followed by several suggested answers or completions. Select the one that BEST answers the question or completes the statement. *PRINT THE LETTER OF THE CORRECT ANSWER IN THE SPACE AT THE RIGHT.*

1. One of the things that can ruin morale in a work group is the failure to exercise judgment in the assignment of overtime work to your subordinates.
   Of the following, the MOST desirable supervisory practice in assigning overtime work is to

   A. *rotate* overtime on a uniform basis among all your subordinates
   B. *assign* overtime to those who are *moonlighting* after regular work hours
   C. *rotate* overtime as much as possible among employees willing to work additional hours
   D. *assign* overtime to those employees who take frequent long weekend vacations

   1.____

2. The consistent delegation of authority by you to experienced and reliable subordinates in your work group is generally considered

   A. *undesirable,* because your authority in the group may be threatened by an unscrupulous subordinate
   B. *undesirable,* because it demonstrates that you cannot handle your own workload
   C. *desirable,* because it shows that you believe that you have been accepted by your subordinates
   D. *desirable,* because the development of subordinates creates opportunities for assuming broader responsibilities yourself

   2.____

3. The MOST effective way for you to deal with a false rumor circulating among your subordinates is to

   A. have a trusted subordinate state a counter-rumor
   B. recommend disciplinary action against the *rumor mongers*
   C. point out to your subordinates that rumors degrade both listener and initiator
   D. furnish your subordinates with sufficient authentic information

   3.____

4. Two of your subordinates tell you about a mistake they made in a report that has already been sent the top management.
   Which of the following questions is *most likely* to elicit the MOST valuable information from your subordinates?

   A. Who is responsible?
   B. How can we explain this to top management?
   C. How did it happen?
   D. Why weren't you more careful?

   4.____

5. Assume that you are responsible for implementing major changes in work flow patterns and personnel assignments in the unit of which you are in charge.
   The *one* of the following actions which is *most likely* to secure the willing cooperation of those persons who will have to change their assignmentsis

   5.____

A. having the top administrators of the agency urge their cooperation at a group meeting
B. issuing very detailed and carefully planned instructions to the affected employees regarding the changes
C. integrating employee participation into the planning of the changes
D. reminding the affected employees that career advancement depends upon compliance with organizational objectives

6. Of the following, the BEST reason for using face-to-face communication *instead of* written communication is that face-to-face communication

   A. allows for immediate feedback
   B. is more credible
   C. enables greater use of detail and illustration
   D. is more polite

7. Of the following, the *most likely* DISADVANTAGE of giving detailed instructions when assigning a task to a subordinate is that such instructions may

   A. conflict with the subordinate's ideas of how the task should be done
   B. reduce standardization of work performance
   C. cause confusion in the mind of the subordinate
   D. inhibit the development of new procedures by the subordinate

8. Assume that you are a supervisor of a unit consisting of a number of subordinates and that one subordinate, whose work is otherwise acceptable, keeps on making errors in one particular task assigned to him in rotation. This task consists of routine duties which all your subordinates should be able to perform.
    Of the following, the BEST way for you to handle this situation is to

   A. do the task yourself when the erring employee is scheduled to perform it and assign this employee other duties
   B. reorganize work assignments so that the task in question is no longer performed in rotation but assigned full-time to your most capable subordinate
   C. find out why this subordinate keeps on making the errors in question and see that he learns how to do the task properly
   D. maintain a well-documented record of such errors and, when the evidence is overwhelming, recommend appropriate disciplinary action

9. In the past, Mr. T, one of your subordinates, had been generally withdrawn and suspicious of others, but he had produced acceptable work. However, Mr. T has lately started to get into arguments with his fellow workers during which he displays intense rage. Friction between this subordinate and the others in your unit is mounting and the unit's work is suffering.
    Of the following, which would be the BEST way for you to handle this situation?

   A. Rearrange work schedules and assignments so as to give Mr. T no cause for complaint
   B. Instruct the other workers to avoid Mr. T and not to respond to any abuse
   C. Hold a unit meeting and appeal for harmony and submergence of individual differences in the interest of work
   D. Maintain a record of incidents and explore with Mr. T the possibility of seeking professional help

10. You are responsible for seeing to it that your unit is functioning properly in the accomplishment of its budgeted goals.
Which of the following will provide the LEAST information on how well you are accomplishing such goals?

    A. Measurement of employee performance
    B. Identification of alternative goals
    C. Detection of employee errors
    D. Preparation of unit reports

10._____

11. Some employees see an agency training program as a threat. Of the following, the *most likely* reason for such an employee attitude toward training is that the employee involved feel that

    A. some trainers are incompetent
    B. training rarely solves real work-a-day problems
    C. training may attempt to change comfortable behavior patterns
    D. training sessions are boring

11._____

12. Of the following, the CHIEF characteristic which distinguishes a *good* supervisor from a *poor* supervisor is the *good* supervisor's

    A. ability to favorably impress others
    B. unwillingness to accept monotony or routine
    C. ability to deal constructively with problem situations
    D. strong drive to overcome opposition

12._____

13. Of the following, the MAIN disadvantage of on-the-job training is that, *generally,*

    A. special equipment may be needed
    B. production may be slowed down
    C. the instructor must maintain an individual relationship with the trainee
    D. the on-the-job instructor must be better qualified than the classroom instructor

13._____

14. All of the following are *correct* methods for a supervisor to use in connection with employee discipline EXCEPT

    A. trying not to be too lenient or too harsh
    B. informing employees of the rules and the penalties for violations of the rules
    C. imposing discipline immediately after the violation is discovered
    D. making sure, when you apply discipline, that the employee understands that you do not want to do it

14._____

15. Of the following, the MAIN reason for a supervisor to establish standard procedures for his unit is to

    A. increase the motivation for his subordinates
    B. make it easier for the subordinates to submit to authority
    C. reduce the number of times that his subordinates have to consult him
    D. reduce the number of mistakes that his subordinates will make

15._____

16. Of the following, the BEST reason for using form letters in correspondence is that they are 16.____

    A. concise and businesslike
    B. impersonal in tone
    C. uniform in appearance
    D. economical for large mailings

17. The use of loose-leaf office manuals for the guidance of employees on office policy, organization, and office procedures has won wide acceptance. 17.____
    The MAIN advantage of the loose-leaf format is that it

    A. allows speedy reference
    B. facilitates revisions and changes
    C. includes a complete index
    D. presents a professional appearance

18. Office forms sometimes consist of several copies, each of a different color. 18.____
    The MAIN reason for using *different* colors is to

    A. make a favorable impression on the users of the form
    B. distinguish each copy from the others
    C. facilitate the preparation of legible carbon copies
    D. reduce cost, since using colored stock permits recycling of paper

19. Which of the following is the BEST justification for obtaining a photocopying machine for the office? 19.____

    A. A photocopying machine can produce an unlimited number of copies at a low fixed cost per copy.
    B. Employees need little training in operating a photocopying machine.
    C. Office costs will be reduced and efficiency increased.
    D. The legibility of a photocopy generally is superior to copy produced by any other office duplicating device.

20. Which one of the following should be the most IMPORTANT overall consideration when preparing a recommendation to automate a large-scale office activity? 20.____
    The

    A. number of models of automated equipment available
    B. benefits and costs of automation
    C. fears and resistance of affected employees
    D. experience of offices which have automated similar activities

21. A tickler file is MOST appropriate for filing materials 21.____

    A. chronologically according to date they were received
    B. alphabetically by name
    C. alphabetically by subject
    D. chronologically according to date they should be followed up

22. Which of the following is the BEST reason for decentralizing rather than centralizing the use of duplicating machines?   22.____

    A. Developing and retaining efficient deplicating machine operators
    B. Facilitating supervision of duplicating services
    C. Motivating employees to produce legible duplicated copies
    D. Placing the duplicating machines where they are most convenient and most frequently used

23. Window envelopes are sometimes considered preferable to individually addressed envelopes PRIMARILY because   23.____

    A. window envelopes are available in standard sizes for all purposes
    B. window envelopes are more attractive and official-looking
    C. the use of window envelopes eliminates the risk of inserting a letter in the wrong envelope
    D. the use of window envelopes requires neater typing

24. In planning the layout of a new office, the utilization of space and the arrangement of staff, furnishings and equipment should *usually* be MOST influenced by the   24.____

    A. gross square footage
    B. status differences in the chain of command
    C. framework of informal relationships among employees
    D. activities to be performed

25. When delegating responsibility for an assignment to a subordinate, it is MOST important that you   25.____

    A. retain all authority necessary to complete the assignment
    B. make your self generally available for consultation with the subordinate
    C. inform your superiors that you are no longer responsible for the assignment
    D. decrease the number of subordinates whom you have to supervise

---

KEY (CORRECT ANSWERS)

1.	C	11.	C	21.	D
2.	D	12.	C	22.	D
3.	D	13.	B	23.	C
4.	D	14.	D	24.	D
5.	C	15.	C	25.	B
6.	A	16.	D		
7.	D	17.	B		
8.	C	18.	B		
9.	D	19.	C		
10.	B	20.	B		

TEST 2

DIRECTIONS: Each question or incomplete statement is followed by several suggested answers or completions. Select the one that BEST answers the question or completes the statement. *PRINT THE LETTER OF THE CORRECT ANSWER IN THE SPACE AT THE RIGHT.*

Questions 1-5.

DIRECTIONS: Answer Questions 1 through 5 on the basis of the following passage.

The most effective control mechanism to prevent gross incompetence on the part of public employees is a good personnel program. The personnel officer in the line departments and the central personnel agency should exert positive leadership to raise levels of performance. Although the key factor is the quality of the personnel recruited, staff members other than personnel officers can make important contributions to efficiency. Administrative analysts, now employed in many agencies, make detailed studies of organization and procedures, with the purpose of eliminating delays, waste, and other inefficiencies. Efficiency is, however, more than a question of good organization and procedures; it is also the product of the attitudes and values of the public employees. Personal motivation can provide the will to be efficient. The best management studies will not result in substantial improvement of the performance of those employees who feel no great urge to work up to their abilities.

1. The passage indicates that the *key* factor in preventing gross incompetence of public employees is the

   A. hiring of administrative analysts to assist personnel people
   B. utilization of effective management studies
   C. overlapping of responsibility
   D. quality of the employees hired

1._____

2. According to the above passage, the central personnel agency staff *should*

   A. work more closely with administrative analysts in the line departments than with personnel afficers
   B. make a serious effort to avoid jurisdictional conflicts with personnel officers in line departments
   C. contribute to improving the quality of work of public employees
   D. engage in a comprehensive program to change the public's negative image of public employees

2._____

3. The passage indicates that efficiency in an organization can BEST be brought about by

   A. eliminating ineffective control mechanisms
   B. instituting sound organizational procedures
   C. promoting competent personnel
   D. recruiting people with desire to do good work

3._____

4. According to the passage, the *purpose* of administrative analysis in a public agency is to

   A. prevent injustice to the public employee
   B. promote the efficiency of the agency
   C. protect the interests of the public
   D. ensure the observance of procedural due process

4._____

5. The passage implies that a considerable rise in the quality of work of public employees   5.____
can be brought about by

    A. encouraging positive employee attitudes toward work
    B. controlling personnel officers who exceed their powers
    C. creating warm personal associations among public employees in an agency
    D. closing loopholes in personnel organization and procedures

6. Typist *X* can type 20 forms per hour and Typist *I* can type 30 forms per hour.   6.____
If there are 30 forms to be typed and both typists are put to work on the job, *how soon*
should they be expected to finish the work? _____ minutes.

    A. 32   B. 34   C. 36   D. 38

7. Assume that there were 18 working days in February and that the six clerks in your unit   7.____
had the following number of absences:

        Clerk F - 3 absences
        Clerk G - 2 absences
        Clerk H - 8 absences
        Clerk I - 1 absence
        Clerk J - 0 absences
        Clerk K - 5 absences

The average percentage attendance for the six clerks in your unit in February was,
most nearly,

    A. 80%   B. 82%   C. 84%   D. 86%

8. A certain employee is paid at the rate of $7.50 per hour, with time-and-a-half for over-   8.____
time. Hours in excess of 40 hours a week count as overtime. During the past week the
employee put in 48 working hours.
The employee's gross wages for the week are, *most nearly,*

    A. $330   B. $350   C. $370   D. $390

9. You are making a report on the number of inside and outside calls handled by a particu-   9.____
lar switchboard. Over a 15-day period, the total number of all inside and outside calls
handled by the switchboard was 5,760. The average number of inside calls per day was
234. You cannot find one day's tally of outside calls, but the total number of outside calls
for the other fourteen days was 2,065. From this information, how many *outside calls*
must have been reported on the missing tally?

    A. 175   B. 185   C. 195   D. 205

10. A floor plan has been prepared for a new building, drawn to a scale of 3/4 inch = 1 foot. A   10.____
certain area is drawn 1 and 1/2 feet long and 6 inches wide on the floor plan. What are
the *actual* dimensions of this area in the new building? _____ feet long and _____ feet
wide.

    A. 21; 8   B. 24; 8   C. 27; 9   D. 30; 9

Questions 11 - 15.

DIRECTIONS: In answering Questions 11 through 15, assume that you are in charge of public information for an office which issues reports and answers questions from
other offices and from the public on changes in land use. The charts below
represent comparative land use in four neighborhoods. The area of each
neighborhood is expressed in city blocks. Assume that all city blocks are the
same size.

NEIGHBORHOOD A - 16 CITY BLOCKS

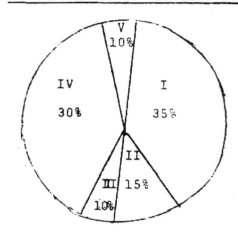

NEIGHBORHOOD B - 24 CITY BLOCKS

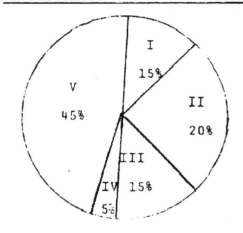

NEIGHBORHOOD C - 20 CITY BLOCKS

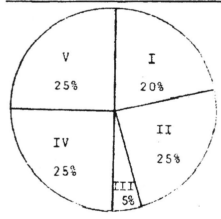

NEIGHBORHOOD D - 12 CITY BLOCKS

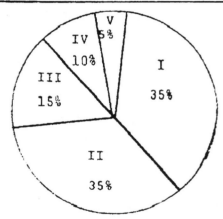

KEY: I- one- and two-family houses   III. Office buildings
       II- Apartment buildings   IV. Rental stores
                   V. Factories and warehouses

11.   In how many of these neighborhoods does residential use (categories I and II together)   11._____
      account for at least 50% of the land use?

      A.   One   B.   Two   C.   Three   D.   Four

12.   Which neighborhood has the largest land area occupied by apartment buildings? Neigh-   12._____
      borhood _____ .

      A.   A   B.   B   C.   C   D.   D

13. In which neighborhood is the largest percentage of the land devoted to both office buildings and retail stores? Neighborhood _____ .   13._____

    A. A   B. B   C. C   D. D

14. What is the difference, to the nearest city block, between the amount of land devoted to retail stores in Neighborhood B and the amount devoted to similar use in Neighborhood C? _____ block(s).   14._____

    A. 1   B. 2   C. 4   D. 6

15. Which one of the following types of buildings occupies the same amount of land area in Neighborhood B as the amount of land area occupied by retail stores in Neighborhood A?   15._____

    A.   Factories and warehouses
    B.   Office buildings
    C.   Retail stores
    D.   Apartment buildings

Questions 16 - 20.

DIRECTIONS: Answer Questions 16 through 20 on the basis of the following passage.

For a period of nearly fifteen years, beginning in the mid-1950's, higher education sustained a phenomenal rate of growth. The factors principally responsible were continuing improvement in the rate of college entrance by high school graduates, a 50-percent increase in the size of the college-age (eighteen to twenty-one) group, and - until about 1967 - a rapid expansion of university research activity supported by the federal government.

Today, as one looks ahead fifteen years to the year 2020, it is apparent that each of these favorable stimuli will either be abated or turn into a negative factor. The rate of growth of the college-age group has already diminished, and from 2010 to 2015 the size of the college-age group will shrink annually almost as fast as it grew from 1965 to 1970. From 2015 to 2020, this annual decrease will slow down so that by 2020 the age-group will be about the same size as it was in 2019. This substantial net decrease in the size of the college-age group over the next fifteen years will dramatically affect college enrollments since, currently, 83 percent of undergraduates are twenty-one and under, and another 11 percent are twenty-one to twenty-four.

16. Which one of the following factors is NOT mentioned in the above passage as contrituting to the high rate of growth of higner education?   16._____

    A.   A larger increase in the size of the eighteen to twenty-one age group
    B.   The equalization of educational opportunities among socio-economic groups
    C.   The federal budget impact on research and development spending in the higher education sector
    D.   The increasing rate at which high school graduates enter college

17. Based on the information in the above passage, the size of the college-age group in 2020 will be

    17.____

    A. larger than it was in 2019
    B. larger than it was in 2005
    C. smaller than it was in 2015
    D. about the same as it was in 2010

18. According to the above passage, the tremendous rate of growth of higher education started around

    18.____

    A. 1950   B. 1955   C. 1960   D. 1965

19. The percentage of undergraduates who are over age 24 is, *most nearly,*

    19.____

    A. 6%   B. 8%   C. 11%   D. 17%

20. Which one of the following conclusions can be substantiated by the information given in the above passage?

    20.____

    A. The college-age group will be about the same size in 2010 as it was in 1965.
    B. The annual decrease in the size of the college-age group from 2010 to 2015 will be about the same as the annual increase from 1965 to 1970.
    C. The overall decrease in the size of the college-age group from 2010 to 2015 will be followed by an overall increase in its size from 2015 to 2020.
    D. The size of the college-age group will decrease at a fairly constant rate from 1995 to 2010.

21. Because higher status is important to many employees, they will often make an effort to achieve it as an end in itself.
    Of the following, the BEST course of action for the supervisor to take on the basis of the preceding statement is to

    21.____

    A. attach higher status to that behavior of subordinates which is directed toward reaching the goals of the organization
    B. avoid showing sympathy toward subordinates' wishes for increased wages, improved working conditions, or other benefits
    C. foster interpersonal competitiveness among subordinates so that personal friendliness is replaced by the desire to protect individual status
    D. reprimand subordinates whenever their work is in some way unsatisfactory in order to adjust their status accordingly

22. Assume that a large office in a certain organization operates long hours and is thus on two shifts with a slight overlap. Those employees, including supervisors, who are most productive are given their choice of shifts. The earlier shift is considered preferable by most employees .
    As a result of this method of assignment, which of the following is *most likely* to result?

    22.____

    A. Most non-supervisory employees will be assigned to the late shift; most supervisors will be assigned to the early shift.
    B. Most supervisors will be assigned to the late shift; most non-supervisory employees will be assigned to the early shift.
    C. The early shift will be more productive than the late shift.
    D. The late shift will be more productive than the early shift.

23. Assume that a supervisor of a unit in which the employees are of avera.ge friendliness   23.____
tells a newly-hired employee on her first day that her co-workers are very friendly. The
other employees hear his remarks to the new employee.
Which of the following is the most *likely* result of this action of the supervisor? The

    A. newly-hired employee will tend to feel less friendly than if the supervisor had said
       nothing
    B. newly-hired employee will tend to believe that her co-workers are very friendly
    C. other employees will tend to feel less friendly toward one another
    D. other employees will tend to see the newly-hired employee as insincerely friendly

24. A recent study of employee absenteeism showed that, although unscheduled absence   24.____
for part of a week is relatively high for young employees, unscheduled absence for a full
week is low. However, although full-week unscheduled absence is least frequent for the
youngest employees, the frequency of such absence increases as the age of employees
increases.
Which of the following statements is the MOST logical explanation for the greater full-
week absenteeism among older employees?

    A. *Older* employees are more likely to be males.
    B. *Older* employees are more likely to have more relatively serious illnesses.
    C. *Younger* employees are more likely to take longer vacations.
    D. *Younger* employees are more likely to be newly-hired.

25. An employee can be motivated to fulfill his needs as he sees them. He is not motivated   25.____
by what others think he ought to have, but what he himself wants. Which of the following
statements follows MOST logically from the foregoing viewpoint?

    A. A person's different traits may be separately classified, but they are all part of one
       system comprising a whole person.
    B. Every job, however simple, entitles the person who does it to proper respect and
       recognition of his unique aspirations and abilities.
    C. No matter what equipment and facilities an organization has, they cannot be put to
       use except by people who have been motivated.
    D. To an observer, a person's need may be unrealistic but they are still controlling.

KEY (CORRECT ANSWERS)

1.	D		11.	B
2.	C		12.	C
3.	D		13.	A
4.	B		14.	C
5.	A		15.	D
6.	C		16.	B
7.	B		17.	C
8.	D		18.	B
9.	B		19.	A
10.	B		20.	B

21. A
22. C
23. B
24. B
25. D

_____

EXAMINATION SECTION
TEST 1

DIRECTIONS: Each question or incomplete statement is followed by several suggested answers or completions. Select the one that BEST answers the question or completes the statement. *PRINT THE LETTER OF THE CORRECT ANSWER IN THE SPACE AT THE RIGHT.*

1. Assume that you are a supervisor of a unit which is about to start work on an urgent job. One of your subordinates starts to talk to you about the urgent job but seems not to be saying what is really on his mind.
   What is the BEST thing for you to say under these circumstances?

   A. *I'm not sure I understand. Can you explain that?*
   B. *Please come to the point. We haven't got all day.*
   C. *What is it? Can't you see I'm busy?*
   D. *Haven't you got work to do? What do you want?*

   1.____

2. Assume that you have recently been assigned a new subordinate. You have explained to this subordinate how to fill out certain forms which will constitute the major portion of her job. After the first day, you find that she has filled out the forms correctly but has not completed as many as most other workers normally complete in a day.
   Of the following, the MOST appropriate action for you to take is to

   A. tell the subordinate how many forms she is expected to complete
   B. instruct the subordinate in the correct method of filling out the forms
   C. monitor the subordinate's production to see if she improves
   D. reassign the job of filling out the forms to a more experienced worker in the unit

   2.____

3. One of the problems commonly met by the supervisor is the *touchy* employee who imagines slights when none are intended.
   Of the following, the BEST way to deal with such an employee is to

   A. ignore him, until he sees the error of his behavior
   B. frequently reassure him of his value as a person
   C. advise him that oversensitive people rarely get promoted
   D. issue written instructions to him to avoid misinterpretation

   3.____

4. The understanding supervisor should recognize that a certain amount of anxiety is common to all newly-hired employees. If you are a supervisor of a unit and a newly-hired employee has been assigned to you, you can usually assume that the LEAST likely worry that the new employee has is worry about

   A. the job and the standards required in the job
   B. his acceptance by the other people in your unit
   C. the difficulty of advancing to top positions in the agency
   D. your fairness in evaluating his work

   4.____

5. In assigning work to subordinates, it is often desirable for you to tell them the overall or ultimate objective of the assignment.
Of the following, the BEST reason for telling them the objective is that it will

    A. assure them that you know what you are doing
    B. eliminate most of the possible complaints about the assignment
    C. give them confidence in their ability to do the assignment
    D. help them to make decisions consistent with the objective

5.____

6. Generally a supervisor wishes to increase the likelihood that instructions given to subordinates will be carried out properly.
Of the following, the MOST important action for the supervisor to take to accomplish this objective when giving instructions to subordinates is to

    A. tailor the instructions to fit the interests of the subordinate
    B. use proper timing in giving the instruction
    C. make sure that the subordinates understand the instructions
    D. include only those instructions that are essential to the task at hand

6.____

7. Suppose that a supervisor, because of his heavy workload, has decided to delegate to his subordinates some of the duties that he has been performing.
Of the following attitudes of the supervisor, the one that is LEAST conducive toward effective delegation is his belief that

    A. his subordinates will make some mistakes in performing these duties
    B. controls will be necessary to make sure the work is done
    C. performance of these duties may be slowed down temporarily
    D. much of his time will be spent supervising performance of these duties

7.____

8. In attempting to determine why one of his subordinates has frequently been coming to work late, a supervisor begins an interview with the subordinate by asking her whether everything is all right on the job and at home. The BEST of the following reasons for beginning the interview in this manner is that a question specifically about the reason for the lateness

    A. might indicate insecurity on the part of the supervisor
    B. might limit the responses of the subordinate
    C. will offend the subordinate
    D. might reveal the purpose of the interview

8.____

9. Of the following, the BEST use to which a supervisor should put his knowledge of human relations is to

    A. enhance his image among his subordinates
    B. improve interpersonal relationships with the organization
    C. prompt the organization to an awareness of mental health
    D. resolve technical differences of opinion among employees

9.____

10. Which of the following types of information would come tribute LEAST to a measure of the quality of working conditions for employees in various jobs?

    A. Data reflecting a view of working conditions as seen through the eyes of workers
    B. Objective data relating to problems in working conditions, such as occupational safety statistics
    C. The considered opinion of recognized specialists in relevant fields
    D. The impressionistic accounts of journalists in feature articles

10.____

Questions 11–15

DIRECTIONS: Questions 11 through 15 each consist of a sentence which may or may not be an example of good English usage. Consider grammar, punctuation, spelling, capitalization, verbosity, awkwardness, etc. Examine each sentence, and then choose the correct statement about it from the four choices below it. If the English usage in the sentence is better as given than with any of the changes suggested in options B, C, or D, choose option A. Do NOT choose an option that will change the meaning of the sentence.

11. The clerk could have completed the assignment on time if he knows where these materials were located.

    A. This is an example of acceptable writing.
    B. The word *knows* should be replaced by *had known*.
    C. The word *were* should be replaced by *had been*.
    D. The words *where these materials were located* should be replaced by *the location of these materials*.

11.____

12. All employees should be given safety training. Not just those who have accidents.

    A. This is an example of acceptable writing.
    B. The period after the word *training* should be changed to a colon.
    C. The period after the word *training* should be changed to a semicolon, and the first letter of the word *Not* should be changed to a small *n*.
    D. The period after the word *training* should be changed to a comma, and the first letter of the word *Not* should be changed to a small *n*.

12.____

13. This proposal is designed to promote employee awareness of the suggestion program, to encourage employee participation in the program, and to increase the number of suggestions submitted.

    A. This is an example of acceptable writing.
    B. The word *proposal* should be spelled *preposal*.
    C. the words *to increase the number of suggestions submitted* should be changed to *an increase in the number of suggestions is expected*.
    D. The word *promote* should be changed to *enhance* and the word *increase* should be changed to *add to*.

13.____

14. The introduction of inovative managerial techniques should be preceded by careful anal-   14.____
    ysis of the specific circumstances and conditions in each department.

    A. This is an example of acceptable writing.
    B. The word *techniques* should be spelled *techneques*.
    C. The word *inovative* should be spelled *innovative*.
    D. A comma should be placed after the word *circumstance* and after the word *conditions*.

15. This occurrence indicates that such criticism embarrasses him.   15.____

    A. This is an example of acceptable writing.
    B. The word *occurrence* should be spelled *occurence*.
    C. The word *criticism* should be spelled *criticizm*.
    D. The word *embarrasses* should be spelled *embarasses*.

Questions 16–18.

DIRECTIONS: Questions 16 through 18 each consist of four sentences. Choose the one sentence in each set of four that would be BEST for a *formal* letter or report. Consider grammar and appropriate usage.

16. A. Most all the work he completed before he become ill.   16.____
    B. He completed most of the work before becoming ill.
    C. Prior to him becoming ill his work was mostly completed.
    D. Before he became ill most of the work he had completed.

17. A. Being that the report lacked a clearly worded recomendation, it did not matter that   17.____
       it contained enough information.
    B. There was enough information in the report, although it, including the recommendation, were not clearly worded.
    C. Although the report contained enough information, it did not have a clearly worded recommendation.
    D. Though the report did not have a recommendation that was clearly worded, and the information therein contained was enough.

18. A. Having already overlooked the important mistakes, the ones which she found were   18.____
       not as important toward the end of the letter.
    B. Toward the end of the letter she had already overlooked the important mistakes, so that which she had found were not as important.
    C. The mistakes which she had already overlooked were not as important as those which near the end of letter she had found.
    D. The mistakes which she found near the end of the letter were not as important as those which she had already overlooked.

19. Examine the following sentence, and then choose from below the words which should be   19.____
    inserted in the blank spaces to produce the best sentence.
       The unit has exceeded _____ goals and the employees are satisfied
       with _____ accomplishments.

    A. their, it's   B. it's, it's
    C. its, there   D. its, their

20. Examine the following sentence, and then choose from below the words which should be inserted in the blank spaces to produce the best sentence.   20.____

      Research indicates that employees who _____ no opportunity for close social relationships often find their work unsatisfying, and this _____ of satisfaction often reflects itself in low production.

    A. have, lack   B. have, excess
    C. has, lack   D. has, excess

KEY (CORRECT ANSWERS)

1.	A		11.	B
2.	C		12.	D
3.	B		13.	A
4.	C		14.	C
5.	D		15.	A
6.	C		16.	B
7.	D		17.	C
8.	B		18.	D
9.	B		19.	D
10.	D		20.	A

TEST 2

DIRECTIONS: Each question or incomplete statement is followed by several suggested answers or completions. Select the one that BEST answers the question or completes the statement. *PRINT THE LETTER OF THE CORRECT ANSWER IN THE SPACE AT THE RIGHT.*

1. Of the following, the GREATEST *pitfall* in interviewing is that the result may be effected by the

    A. bias of the interviewee
    B. bias of the interviewer
    C. educational level of the interviewee
    D. educational level of the interviewer

1.____

2. Assume that you have been asked to interview each of several students who have been hired to work part-time. Which of the following could *ordinarily* be accomplished LEAST effectively in such an interview?

    A. Providing information about the organization or institution in which the students will be working
    B. Directing the students to report for work each afternoon at specified times
    C. Determining experience and background of the students so that appropriate assignments can be made
    D. Changing the attitudes of the students toward the importance of parental controls

2.____

3. Assume that someone you are interviewing is reluctant to give you certain information. He would *probably* be MORE responsive if you show him that

    A. all the other persons you interviewed provided you with the information
    B. it would serve his own best interests to give you the information
    C. the information is very important to you
    D. you are businesslike and take a no-nonsense approach

3.____

4. Taking notes while you are interviewing someone is *most likely* to

    A. arouse doubts as to your trustworthiness
    B. give the interviewee confidence in your ability
    C. insure that you record the facts you think are important
    D. make the responses of the interviewee unreliable

4.____

5. Assume that you have been asked to get all the pertinent information from an employee who claims that she witnessed a robbery.
Which of the following questions is LEAST likely to influence the witness's response?

    A. *Can you describe the robber's hair?*
    B. *Did the robber have a lot of hair?*
    C. *Was the robber's hair black or brown?*
    D. *Was the robber's hair very dark?*

5.____

6. If you are to interview several applicants for jobs and rate them on five different factors on a scale of 1 to 5, you should be MOST careful to *insure* that your   6.____

    A. rating on one factor does not influence your rating on another factor
    B. ratings on all factors are interrelated with a minimum of variation
    C. overall evaluation for employment exactly reflects the arithmetic average of your ratings
    D. overall evaluation for employment is unrelated to your individual ratings

7. In answering questions asked by students, faculty, and the public, it is MOST important that   7.____

    A. you indicate your source of information
    B. you are not held responsible for the answers
    C. the facts you give be accurate
    D. the answers cover every possible aspect of each question

8. One of the applicants for a menial job is a tall, stooped, husky individual with a low fore-head, narrow eyes, a protruding chin, and a tendency to keep his mouth open.
    In interviewing him, you *should*   8.____

    A. check him more carefully than the other applicants regarding criminal background
    B. disregard any skills he might have for other jobs which are vacant
    C. make your vocabulary somewhat simpler than with the other applicants
    D. make no assumption regarding his ability on the basis of his appearance

9. Of the following, the BEST approach for you to use at the beginning of an interview with a job applicant is to   9.____

    A. caution him to use his time economically and to get to the point
    B. ask him how long he intends to remain on the job if hired
    C. make some pleasant remarks to put him at ease
    D. emphasize the importance of the interview in obtaining the job

10. Of the following, the BEST reason for conducting an *exit interview* with an employee is to   10.____

    A. make certain that he returns all identification cards and office keys
    B. find out why he is leaving
    C. provide a useful training device for the exit interviewer
    D. discover if his initial hiring was in error

11. Suppose that a visitor to an office asks a receptionist for a specific person by name. The person is available, but the visitor refuses to state the purpose of the visit, saying that it is *personal.*
    Which of the following is the MOST appropriate response for the receptionist to make?   11.____

    A. *Does M_____ know you?*
    B. *I'm sorry, M_____ is busy.*
    C. *M _____ won't be able to help you unless you're more specific.*
    D. *M_____ is not able to see you.*

12. When writing a reply to a letter you received, it is proper to mention the subject of the letter.
However, you should ordinarily NOT summarize the contents or repeat statements
made in the letter you received PRIMARILY because

    A. a letter writer answers people, not letters
    B. direct answers will help you avoid sounding pompous
    C. the response will thus be more confidential
    D. the sender usually knows what he or she wrote

12._____

13. Assume that you are a supervisor in an office which gets approximately equal quantities
of urgent work and work that is not urgent. The volume of work is high during some periods and low during others.
In order to level out the fluctuations in workload, it would be BEST for you to schedule
work so that

    A. urgent work which comes up in a period of high work volume can be handled expe-
ditiously by the use of voluntary overtime
    B. urgent work is postponed for completion in periods of low volume
    C. work is completed as it comes into the office, except that when urgent work arises,
other work is laid aside temporarily
    D. work is completed chronologically, that is, on the basis of *first in, first out*

13._____

14. Suppose that a supervisor sets up a pick-up and delivery messenger system to cover
several nearby buildings. Each building has at least one station for both pick-up and
delivery. Three messenger trips are scheduled for each day, and the messenger is
instructed to make pick-ups and deliveries at the same time.
In this situation, telling the messenger to visit each pick-up and delivery station even
though there is nothing to deliver to it is

    A. *advisable,* messengers are generally not capable of making decisions for them-
selves
    B. *advisable,* there may be material for the messenger to pick up
    C. *inadvisable,* the system must be made flexible to meet variable workload condi-
tions
    D. *inadvisable,* postponing the visit until there is something to deliver is more efficient

14._____

15. You, as a unit head, have been asked to submit budget estimates of staff, equipment and
supplies in terms of programs for your unit for the coming fiscal year. In addition to their
use in planning, such unit budget estimates can be BEST used to

    A. reveal excessive costs in operations
    B. justify increases in the debt limit
    C. analyze employee salary adjustments
    D. predict the success of future programs

15._____

Questions 16–21.

DIRECTIONS: Questions 16 through 21 involve calculations of annual grade averages for college students who have just completed their junior year. These averages are to be based on the following table showing the number of credit hours for each student during the year at each of the grade levels: A, B, C, D, and F. How these letter grades may be translated into numerical grades is indicated in the first column of the table.

Grade Value	Credit Hours –Junior Year					
	King	Lewis	Martin	Nonkin	Ottly	Perry
A=95	12	12	9	15	6	3
B=85	9	12	9	12	18	6
C=75	6	6	9	3	3	21
D=65	3	3	3	3	–	–
F=0	–	–	3	–	–	–

Calculating a grade average for an individual student is a 4-step process:
  I.   Multiply each grade value by the number of credit hours for which the student received that grade.
  II. Add these multiplication products for each student.
  III. Add the student's total credit hours.
  IV. Divide the multiplication product total by the total number of credit hours.
  V.   Round the result, if there is a decimal place, to the nearest whole number. A number ending in .5 would be rounded to the next higher number.

EXAMPLE
Using student King's grades as an example, his grade average can be calculated by going through the following four steps:

I.   95 x 12 = 1140   III. 12
     85 x 9   = 765   9
     75 x 6   = 450   6
     65 x 3   = 195   3
      0 x 0   =   0   0
                              30 total credit hours

II. Total   = 2550   IV. Divide 2550 by 30: $\frac{2550}{30}$ = 85 .

King's grade average is 85.
Answer Questions 16 through 21 on the basis of the information given above.

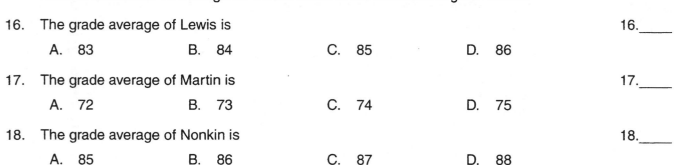

16. The grade average of Lewis is   16.____

    A. 83   B. 84   C. 85   D. 86

17. The grade average of Martin is   17.____

    A. 72   B. 73   C. 74   D. 75

18. The grade average of Nonkin is   18.____

    A. 85   B. 86   C. 87   D. 88

19. Student Ottly must attain a grade average of 90 in each of his years in college to be accepted into the graduate school of his choice.
If, in summer school during his junior year, he takes two 3–credit courses and receives a grade of 95 in each one, his grade average for his junior year will then be, *most nearly,*

   A. 87   B. 88   C. 89   D. 90

19._____

20. If Perry takes an additional 3–credit course during the year and receives a grade of 95, his grade average will be increased to approximately

   A. 79   B. 80   C. 81   D. 82

20._____

21. What has been the *effect* of automation in data processing on the planning of managerial objectives?

   A. Paperwork can be virtually eliminated from the planning process.
   B. The information on which such planning is based can be more precise and up-to-date.
   C. Planning must be done much more frequently because of the constantly changing nature of the objectives.
   D. Planning can be done much less frequently because of the increased stability of objectives.

21._____

22. Which of the following is the BEST reason for budgeting a new calculating machine for an office?

   A. The clerks in the office often make mistakes in adding.
   B. The machine would save time and money.
   C. It was budgeted last year but never received.
   D. All the other offices have calculating machines.

22._____

23. Which of the following is *most likely* to reduce the volume of paperwork in a unit responsible for preparing a large number of reports?

   A. Changing the office layout so that there will be a minimum of backtracking and delay.
   B. Acquiring additional adding and calculating machines.
   C. Consolidating some of the reports.
   D. Inaugurating a *records retention* policy to reduce the length of time office papers are retained.

23._____

24. With regard to typed correspondence received by most offices, which of the following is the GREATEST problem?

   A. Verbosity   B. Illegibility
   C. Improper folding   D. Excessive copies

24._____

25. Of the following, the GREATEST advantage of electronic typewriters over electric type-writers is that they *usually*   25.____

    A. are less expensive to repair
    B. are smaller and lighter
    C. produce better looking copy
    D. require less training for the typist

KEY (CORRECT ANSWERS)

1.	B		11.	A
2.	D		12.	D
3.	B		13.	C
4.	C		14.	B
5.	A		15.	A
6.	A		16.	C
7.	C		17.	D
8.	D		18.	C
9.	C		19.	B
10.	B		20.	B

21.	B
22.	B
23.	C
24.	A
25.	C

EXAMINATION SECTION
TEST 1

DIRECTIONS: Each question or incomplete statement is followed by several suggested answers or completions. Select the one that BEST answers the question or completes the statement. *PRINT THE LETTER OF THE CORRECT ANSWER IN THE SPACE AT THE RIGHT.*

1. If an inch on an office layout drawing equals 4 feet of actual floor dimension, then a room which actually measures 9 feet by 14 feet is represented on the drawing by measurements equalling _____ inches x _____ inches.

    A. 2 1/4; 3 1/2   B. 2 1/2; 3 1/2
    C. 2 1/4; 3 1/4   D. 2 1/2; 3 1/4

    1.____

2. A cooperative education intern works from 1:30 p.m. to 5 p.m. on Mondays, Wednesdays and Fridays, and from 10 a.m. to 2:30 p.m. with no lunch hour on Tuesdays and Thursdays. He earns $7.15 an hour on this job. In addition, he has a Saturday job paying $8.40 an hour at which he works from 9 a.m. to 3 p.m. with a half hour off for lunch. The gross amount that the student earns each week is, MOST nearly,

    A. $160.95   B. $185.60   C. $192.30   D. $208.15

    2.____

3. Thirty-five percent of the College Discovery students who entered community college in 2006 earned an associate degree. Of these students, 89% entered senior college of which 67% went on to earn baccalaureate degrees.
If there were 529 College Discovery students who entered community college in 2006, then the number of those who went on to finally receive a baccalaureate degree is, MOST nearly,

    A. 354   B. 315   C. 124   D. 110

    3.____

4. It takes 5 Office Assistants two days to type 125 letters. Each of the Assistants works at an equal rate of speed. How many days will it take 10 Office Assistants to type 200 letters? _____ day(s).

    A. 1   B. 1 3/5   C. 2   D. 2 1/5

    4.____

5. The following are the grades and credits earned by Student X during the first two years in college

Grade	Credits		Weight	Quality Points
A	10	1/2	x 4	
B	24		x 3	
C	12		x 2	
D	4	1/2	x 1	
F, FW	5		x 0	

To compute an index number:
    I. Multiply the number of credits of each grade by the weight to get the number of *quality points.*
    II. Add the credits.
    III. Add the quality points.
    IV. Divide the total quality points by the total credits, and carry the division to two decimal places.

    5.____

On the basis of the given information, the index number for Student X is

A. 2.54   B. 2.59   C. 2.64   D. 2.68

———

KEY (CORRECT ANSWERS)

1. A
2. B
3. D
4. B
5. A

———

TEST 2

DIRECTIONS: Each question or incomplete statement is followed by several suggested answers or completions. Select the one that BEST answers the question or completes the statement. *PRINT THE LETTER OF THE CORRECT ANSWER IN THE SPACE AT THE RIGHT.*

Questions 1-5.

DIRECTIONS: Answer questions 1 through 5 according to the information given in the graph and chart below.

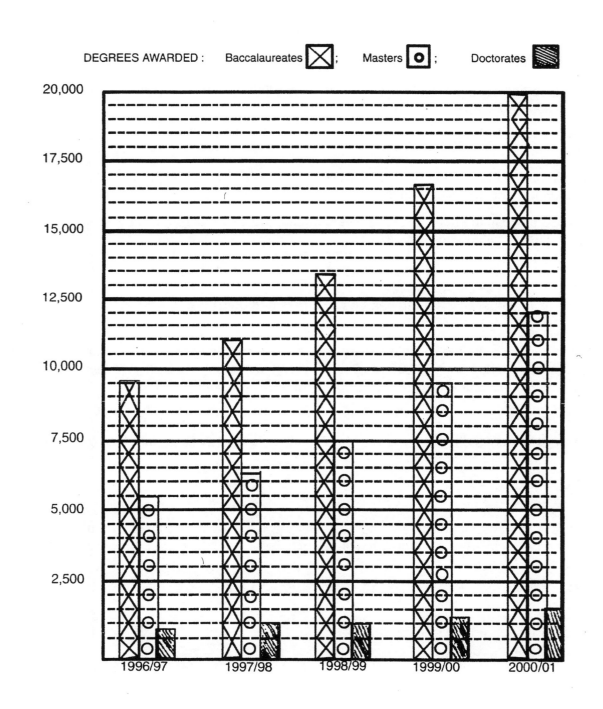

FRESHMAN ENROLLMENTS: BY FIELD

	1998/99		1999/00	
Field	Men	Women	Men	Women
Arts and Sciences	6,296	5,668	7,111	7,110
Engineering	2,098	28	2,370	35
Business	1,574	532	1,777	660
Agriculture	394	59	444	74
Education	1,192	2,272	1,150	2,660
Nursing	65	341	72	450
All Others	2,556	2,465	4,894	3,231
Totals	14,175	11,365	17,818	14,220

1. The data on freshman enrollments by field shows that the female enrollees outnumbered the male enrollees at a ratio of 25:4 in the field of

   A. Engineering in 1998/99
   B. Education in 1998/99
   C. Nursing in 1999/00
   D. Agriculture in 1999/00

1.____

2. In comparing the number of graduate degrees awarded during the five academic years shown, it is correct to state that

   A. the rise in the number of masters degrees awarded was greatest between the years 1999/00 and 2000/01
   B. a yearly average of 1,000 doctorate degrees were awarded
   C. the number of doctorates awarded in 1997/98 was 1/8 the number of masters degrees awarded that year
   D. the number of graduate degrees awarded in 2000/01 was double the number awarded in 1997/98

2.____

3. If the number of baccalaureate degrees awarded increases from 2000/01 to 2001/02 at the same rate as from 1999/00 to 2000/01, then the number of baccalaureate degrees awarded in the academic year 2001/02 would be MOST nearly,

   A. 20,500   B. 22,100   C. 23,800   D. 25,300

3.____

4. In which field of study did the overall freshman enrollment increase just 10% from 1998/99 to 1999/00?

   A. Agriculture
   B. Business
   C. Education
   D. Engineering

4.____

5. If the number of baccalaureate degrees awarded in 1999/00 is equal to 53% of the college entrants in 1996/97, then the number of college entrants in 1996/97 was, MOST nearly,

   A. 17,900   B. 20,210   C. 31,600   D. 35,640

5.____

KEY (CORRECT ANSWERS)

1. C
2. A
3. C
4. C
5. C

TEST 3

Questions 1-5.

1. Insofar as an employee is permitted to *tell off* the boss in public and receives social   1.____
   approval from fellow employees who derive vicarious satisfaction from the employee's
   action, such approval may operate to explain the effectiveness of the boss's authority.

   A. diminish
   C. power
   B. feel
   D. attitude

2. The demand for practical education combined with the prestige denied to purely intellec-   2.____
   tual achievement has produced an educational system that tends to insure the continu-
   ance of education for both purposes.

   A. usefulness
   C. need
   B. accorded
   D. balance

3. Officials in college placement offices have often noted the contradiction which exists   3.____
   between the public statements of the company president who questions the value of a
   general liberal arts education in the business world and the practice of his recruiters who
   seek specialized training for particular jobs.

   A. praises
   C. reject
   B. admissions
   D. pronouncements

4. The difference between an organization as blueprinted and its actuality can be explained   4.____
   by modifications introduced by the people who do the planning of the organization.

   A. similarity
   C. behavior
   B. work
   D. blueprint

5. Students of educational administration have either attempted to accept and analyze the   5.____
   administrative process in their efforts to produce total improvement, or to look in two
   directions away from education, towards substantive educational activity and towards the
   community that supports the organization.

   A. change
   C. administration
   B. failed
   D. ignores

Questions 6-9.

6.   A.   Answering of veterans' inquiries, together with the receipt of fees, have been
          handled by the Bursar's Office since the new President came.
     B.   Since the new President's arrival, the handling of all veteran's inquiries has been
          turned over to the Bursar's Office.
     C.   In addition to the receipt of fees, the Bursar's Office has been handling veterans'
          inquiries since the new President came.
     D.   The principle change in the work of the Bursar's Office since the new President
          came is that it now handles veterans' inquires as well as the receipt of fees.

6.____

7.   A.   The current unrest about education undoubtedly stems in part from the fact that
          the people fear the basic purposes of the schools are being neglected or sup-
          planted by spurious ones.
     B.   The fears of people that the basic purposes of the schools are being neglected
          or supplanted by spurious ones contributes to the current unrest about educa-
          tion.
     C.   Undoubtedly some responsibility for the current unrest about education must be
          assigned to people's fears that the purpose and base of the school system is
          being neglected or supplanted.
     D.   From the fears of people that the basic purposes of the schools one being
          neglected or supplanted by spurious ones undoubtedly stem in part the current
          unrest about education.

7.____

8.   A.   The existence of administrative phenomena are clearly established, but their
          characteristics, relations and laws are obscure.
     B.   The obscurity of the characteristics, relations and laws of administrative phe-
          nomena do not preclude their existence.
     C.   Administrative phenomena clearly exists in spite of the obscurity of their charac-
          teristics, relations and laws.
     D.   The characteristics, relations and laws of administrative phenomena are obscure
          but the existence of the phenomena is clear.

8.____

9.   A.   Though deeply effected by the setback, the advice given by the admissions
          office began to seem more reasonable.
     B.   Although he was deeply effected by the setback, the advice given by the admis-
          sions office began to seem more reasonable.
     C.   Though the setback had affected him deeply, the advice given by the admissions
          office began to seem more reasonable.
     D.   Although he was deeply affected by the setback, the advice given by the admis-
          sions office began to seem more reasonable.

9.____

10.   A. Returning to the administration building after attendance at a meeting, the door   10._____
was locked despite an agreement that is would be left open.
    B. When he returned to the administration building after attending a meeting, he
found the door locked, despite an agreement that it would be left open.
    C. After attending a meeting, the door to the administration building was locked,
despite an agreement that it would be left open.
    D. When he returned to the administration building after attendance at a meeting,
he found the door locked, despite an agreement that it would be left open.

KEY (CORRECT ANSWERS)

1.	A	6.	C
2.	B	7.	A
3.	A	8.	D
4.	B	9.	D
5.	C	10.	B

EXAMINATION SECTION
TEST 1

DIRECTIONS: Each question or incomplete statement is followed by several suggested answers or completions. Select the one that BEST answers the question or completes the statement. *PRINT THE LETTER OF THE CORRECT ANSWER IN THE SPACE AT THE RIGHT.*

1. Of the following methods of conducting an interview, the BEST is to   1.____

   A. ask questions with *yes* or *no* answers
   B. listen carefully and ask only questions that are pertinent
   C. fire questions at the interviewee so that he must answer sincerely and briefly
   D. read standardized questions to the person being interviewed

2. An interviewer should begin with topics which are easy to talk about and which are not threatening.   2.____
   This procedure is useful MAINLY because it

   A. allows the applicant a little time to get accustomed to the situation and leads to freer communication
   B. distracts the attention of the person being interviewed from the main purpose of the questioning
   C. is the best way for the interviewer to show that he is relaxed and confident on the job
   D. causes the interviewee to feel that the interviewer is apportioning valuable questioning time

3. The initial interview will normally be more of a problem to the interviewer than any subsequent interviews he may have with the same person because   3.____

   A. the interviewee is likely to be hostile
   B. there is too much to be accomplished in one session
   C. he has less information about the client than he will have later
   D. some information may be forgotten when later making record of this first interview

4. Most successful interviews are those in which the interviewer shows a genuine interest in the person he is questioning.   4.____
   This attitude would MOST likely cause the individual being interviewed to

   A. feel that the interviewer already knows all the facts in his case
   B. act more naturally and reveal more of his true feelings
   C. request that the interviewer give more attention to his problems, not his personality
   D. react defensively, suppress his negative feelings, and conceal the real facts in his case

5. Questions worded so that the person being interviewed has some hint of the desired answer can modify the person's response.   5.____
   The result of the inclusion of such questions in an interview, even when they are used inadvertently, is to

A. have no effect on the basic content of the information given by the person interviewed
B. have value in convincing the person that the suggested plan is the best for him
C. cause the person to give more meaningful information
D. reduce the validity of the information obtained from the person

6. The person MOST likely to be a good interviewer is one who   6._____

    A. A. is able to outguess the person being interviewed
    B. tries to change the attitudes of the persons he interviews
    C. controls the interview by skillfully dominating the conversation
    D. is able to imagine himself in the position of the person being interviewed

7. The *halo effect* is an overall impression on the interviewer, whether favorable or unfavor-   7._____
able, usually created by a single trait. This impression then influences the appraisal of all
other factors.
A *halo effect* is LEAST likely to be created at an interview where the interviewee is a

    A. person of average appearance and ability
    B. rough-looking man who uses abusive language
    C. young attractive woman being interviewed by a man
    D. person who demonstrates an exceptional ability to remember facts

8. Of the following, the BEST way for an interviewer to calm a person who seems to have   8._____
become emotionally upset as a result of a question asked is for the interviewer to

    A. talk to the person about other things for a short time
    B. ask that the person control himself
    C. probe for the cause of his emotional upset
    D. finish the questioning as quickly as possible

9. Of the following, the BEST reason for discarding an ink cartridge is that   9._____

    A. the print quality is too dark
    B. the print quality is faded
    C. the short edge of the sheet is curled
    D. the finish on the sheet is smooth and shiny

10. Persons whose native language is not English sometimes experience difficulty in com-   10._____
munication when visiting public offices.
The MOST common method used by such persons to overcome the difficulty in communication is to

    A. write in their own language whatever they wish to say
    B. hire a professional interpreter
    C. ask a patrolman for assistance
    D. bring with them an English-speaking friend or relative

Questions 11-20.

DIRECTIONS: In each Question 11 through 20, there is a statement which contains a word (one of those underlined) that is either incorrectly used because it is not in keeping with the meaning the quotation is evidently intended to convey, or is misspelled. There is only one incorrect word in each statement. Of the four underlined words in each question, determine if the first one should be replaced by the word lettered A, the second replaced by the word lettered B, the third replaced by the word lettered C, or the fourth replaced by the word lettered D. Indicate in the space at the right the replacement word you have selected..

11.   Whether one depends on <u>flourescent</u> or artificial light or both, adequate <u>standards</u>   11._____
      should be <u>maintained</u> by means of <u>systematic</u> tests.

    A.   natural   B.   safeguards
    C.   established   D.   routine

12.   A policeman has to be <u>prepared</u> to assume his <u>knowledge</u> as a social <u>scientist</u> in the   12._____
      <u>community</u>.

    A.   forced   B.   role
    C.   philosopher   D.   street

13.   It is <u>practically</u> impossible to <u>tell</u> whether a sentence is very long simply by <u>measuring</u> its   13._____
      length.

    A.   almost   B.   mark   C.   too   D.   denoting

14.   By <u>using</u> carbon paper, the typist <u>easily</u> is able to <u>insert</u> as many as six <u>copies</u> of a   14._____
      report.

    A.   adding   B.   seldom   C.   make   D.   forms

15.   Although all people have many <u>traits</u> in common, a receptionist in her <u>agreements</u> with   15._____
      people <u>learns</u> quickly how <u>different</u> each person is from every other person.

    A.   impressions   B.   associations
    C.   decides   D.   various

16.   Strong <u>leaders</u> are <u>required</u> to organize a community for delinquency prevention and for   16._____
      <u>dissemination</u> of organized crime and drug addiction.

    A.   tactics   B.   important
    C.   control   D.   meetings

17.   The <u>demonstrators</u>, who were taken to the Criminal Courts building in <u>Manhattan</u>   17._____
      (because it was large enough to <u>accommodate</u> them), contended that the arrests were
      <u>unwarrented</u>.

    A.   demonstraters   B.   Manhatten
    C.   accomodate   D.   unwarranted

18.   When two or more forms for spelling a word exist, it is <u>advisable</u> to use the <u>preferred</u>   18._____
      spelling indicated in the <u>dictionary</u>, and to use it <u>consistantly</u>.

    A.   adviseable   B.   prefered
    C.   dictionery   D.   consistently

19. If you know the language of the <u>foreign</u> country you are visiting, your <u>embarassment</u> will   19.____
    <u>disappear</u> and you will learn a lot more about the customs and <u>characteristics</u> of the
    common people.

    A. foriegn   B. embarrassment
    C. dissappear   D. charactaristics

20. Material consisting of government bulletins, <u>adverticements</u>, <u>catalogues,</u> announce-   20.____
    ments of address changes, and any other <u>periodical</u> material of this nature may be filed
    <u>alphabetically</u> according to subject.

    A. advertisements   B. cataloges
    C. periodicle   D. alphabeticly

Questions 21-24.

DIRECTIONS: Each of the two sentences in Questions 21 through 24 may be correct or may
               contain errors in punctuation, capitalization, or grammar.
               If there is an error in only Sentence I, mark your answer A.
               If there is an error in only Sentence II, mark your answer B.
               If there is an error in both Sentence I and Sentence II, mark your answer C.
               If both Sentence I and Sentence II are correct, mark your answer D.

21.   I. It is very annoying to have a pencil sharpener, which is not in proper working   21.____
           order.
       II. The building watchman checked the door of Charlie's office and found that
           the lock has been jammed.

22.   I. Since he went on the City Council a year ago, one of his primary concerns   22.____
           has been safety in the streets.
       II. After waiting in the doorway for about 15 minutes, a black sedan appeared.

23.   I. When you are studying a good textbook is important.   23.____
       II. He said he would divide the money equally between you and me.

24.   I. The question is, "How can a large number of envelopes be sealed rapidly   24.____
           without the use of a sealing machine?"
       II. The administrator assigned two stenographers, Mary and I, to the new
           bureau.

Questions 25-26.

DIRECTIONS: In each of Questions 25 and 26, the four sentences are from a paragraph in a
               report. They are not in the right order. Which of the following arrangements is
               the BEST one?

25.   I.   An executive may answer a letter by writing his reply on the face of the letter   25.____
            itself instead of having a return letter typed.
       II. This procedure is efficient because it saves the executive's time, the typist's
            time, and saves office file space.
       III. Copying machines are used in small offices as well as large offices to save
            time and money in making brief replies to business letters.
       IV. A copy is made on a copying machine to go into the company files, while the
            original is mailed back to the sender.

The CORRECT answer is:

    A. I, II, IV, III   B. I, IV, II, III
    C. III, I, IV, II   D. III, IV,II,I

26.   I.   Most organizations favor one of the types but always include the others to a lesser degree.

        II.   However, we can detect a definite trend toward greater use of symbolic control.

        III. We suggest that our local police agencies are today primarily utilizing material control.

        IV. Control can be classified into three types: physical, material, and symbolic.

The CORRECT answer is:

    A. IV, II, III, I   B. II, I, IV, III
    C. III, IV, II, I   D. IV, I, III, II

27. Of the following, the MOST effective report writing style is usually characterized by

    A. covering all the main ideas in the same paragraph
    B. presenting each significant point in a new paragraph
    C. placing the least important points before the most important points
    D. giving all points equal emphasis throughout the report

28. Of the following, which factor is COMMON to all types of reports?

    A. Presentation of information
    B. Interpretation of findings
    C. Chronological ordering of the information
    D. Presentation of conclusions and recommendations

29. When writing a report, the one of the following which you should do FIRST is

    A. set up a logical work schedule
    B. determine your objectives in writing the report
    C. select your statistical material
    D. obtain the necessary data from the files

30. Generally,the frequency with which reports are to be submitted or the length of the interval which they cover should depend MAINLY on the

    A. amount of time needed to prepare the reports
    B. degree of comprehensiveness required in the reports
    C. availability of the data to be included in the reports
    D. extent of the variations in the data with the passage of time

31. The objectiveness of a report is its unbiased presentation of the facts.
If this is so, which of the following reports listed below is likely to be the MOST objective?

    A. The Best Use of an Electronic Computer in Department Z
    B. The Case for Raising the Salaries of Employees in Department A
    C. Quarterly Summary of Production in the Duplicating Unit of Department Y
    D. Recommendation to Terminate Employee X's Services Because of Misconduct

Questions 32-37.

DIRECTIONS: Questions 32 through 37 are to be answered only on the basis of the information contained in the charts below which relate to the budget allocations of City
X, a small suburban community. The charts depict the annual budget allocations by department and by expenditures over a five-year period

CITY X BUDGET IN MILLIONS OF DOLLARS

TABLE I.   Budget Allocations By Department

Department	1997	1998	1999	2000	2001
Public Safety	30	45	50	40	50
Health and Welfare	50	75	90	60	70
Engineering	5	8	10	5	8
Human Resources	10	12	20	10	22
Conservation and Environment	10	15	20	20	15
Education and Development	15	25	35	15	15
TOTAL BUDGET	120	180	225	150	180

TABLE II.   Budget Allocations by Expenditures

Category	1997	1998	1999	2000	2001
Raw Materials and Machinery	36	63	68	30	98
Capital Outlay	12	27	56	15	18
Personal Services	72	90	101	105	64
TOTAL BUDGET	120	180	225	150	160

32.   The year in which the SMALLEST percentage of the total annual budget was allocated to   32._____
the Department of Education and Development is

A.   1997   B.   1998   C.   2000   D.   2001

33.   Assume that in 2000 the Department of Conservation and Environment divided its   33._____
annual budget into the three categories of expenditures and in exactly the same pro-
portion as the budget shown in Table II for the year 2000. The amount allocated for capi-
tal outlay in the Department of Conservation and Environment's 2000 budget was MOST
NEARLY _____ million.

A. $2   B. $4   C. $6   D. $10

34.   From the year 1998 to the year 2000, the sum of the annual budgets for the Departments   34._____
of Public Safety and Engineering showed an overall _____ of _____ million.

A.   decline; $8   B.   increase; $7
C.   decline; $15   D.   increase; $22

35.   The LARGEST dollar increase in departmental budget allocations from one year to the   35._____
next was in

A.   Public Safety from 1997 to 1998
B.   Health and Welfare from 1997 to 1998
C.   Education and Development from 1999 to 2000
D.   Human Resources from 1999 to 2000

36. During the five-year period, the annual budget of the Department of Human Resources   36.____
was GREATER than the annual budget for the Department of Conservation and Environment in _____ of the years.

    A. none   B. one   C. two   D. three

37. If the total City X budget increases at the same rate from 2001 to 2002 as it did from   37.____
2000 to 2001, the total City X budget for 2002 will be MOST NEARLY _____ million.

    A. $180   B. $200   C. $210   D. $215

Questions 38-44.

DIRECTIONS: Questions 38 through 44 are to be answered ONLY on the basis of the information contained in the graph below, which relates to the work of a public
agency.

No. of work
units completed

Units of each type of work completed by a public agency from 1996
to 2001

Letters written   ——————————   Applications Processed   ——o——o——

Documents filed   —x——x——x——   Inspections Made   oooooooooooooooooo

38. The year for which the number of units of one type of work completed was less than it   38.____
was for the previous year while the number of each of the other types of work completed
was more than it was for the previous year was

    A. 1997   B. 1998   C. 1999   D. 2000

39. The number of letters written exceeded the number of applications processed by the   39.____
same amount in _____ of the years.

    A. two   B. three   C. four   D. five

40. The year in which the number of each type of work completed was GREATER than the preceding year was
40._____

    A. 1998   B. 1999   C. 2000   D. 2001

41. The number of applications processed and the number of documents filed were the same in
41._____

    A. 1997   B. 1998   C. 1999   D. 2000

42. The total number of units of work completed by the agency
42._____

    A. increased in each year after 1996
    B. decreased from the prior year in two of the years after 1996
    C. was the same in two successive years from 1996 to 2001
    D. was less in 1996 than in any of the following years

43. For the year in which the number of letters written was twice as high as it was in 1996, the number of documents filed was
43._____

    A. the same as it was in 1996
    B. two-thirds of what it was in 1996
    C. five-sixths of what it was in 1996
    D. one and one-half times what it was in 1996

44. The variable which was the MOST stable during the period 1996 through 2001 was
44._____

    A. Inspections Made   B. Letters Written
    C. Documents Filed   D. Applications Processed

Questions 45-50.

DIRECTIONS: Questions 45 through 50 are to be answered ONLY on the basis of the information in the following passage.

Job evaluation and job rating systems are intended to introduce scientific procedures. Any type of approach, when properly used, will give satisfactory results. The Point System, when properly validated by actual use, is more likely to be suitable for general use than the ranking system. In many aspects, the Factor Comparison Plan is a point system tied to money values. Of course, there may be another system that combines the ranking system with the point system, especially during the initial stages of the development of the program. After the program has been in use for some time, the tendency is to drop off the ranking phase and continue the use of the point system.

In the ranking system of rating of jobs, every job within the plant is arranged in some order, either from the one with the simplest qualifications to the one with maximum requirements, or in the reverse order. This system should be preceded by careful job analysis and the writing of accurate job descriptions before the rating process is undertaken. It is possible, of course, to take the jobs as they are found in the business enterprise and use the names as they are without any attempt at standardization, and merely rank them according to the general overall impression of the raters. Such a procedure is certain to fall short of what may reasonably be expected of job rating. Another procedure that is in reality merely a modification of the simple rating described above is to establish a series of grades or zones and arrange all the jobs in the plant into groups within these grades and zones. The practice in most common use is to arrange all the jobs in the plant according to their requirements by rating them and then to establish the classifications or groups.

The actual ranking of jobs may be done by one individual, several individuals, or a committee. If several individuals are working independently on the task, it will usually be found that, in general, they agree but that their rankings vary in certain details. A conference between the individuals, with each person giving his reasons why he rated one way or another, usually produces agreement. The detailed job descriptions are particularly helpful when there is disagreement among raters as to the rating of certain jobs. It is not only possible but desirable to have workers participate in the construction of the job description and in rating the job.

45. The MAIN theme of this passage is

45.____

    A. the elimination of bias in job rating
    B. the rating of jobs by the ranking system
    C. the need for accuracy in allocating points in the point system
    D. pitfalls to avoid in selecting key jobs in the Factor Comparison Plan

46. The ranking system of rating jobs consists MAINLY of

46.____

    A. attaching a point value to each ratable factor of each job prior to establishing an equitable pay scale
    B. arranging every job in the organization in descending order and then following this up with a job analysis of the key jobs
    C. preparing accurate job descriptions after a job analysis and then arranging all jobs either in ascending or descending order based on job requirements
    D. arbitrarily establishing a hierarchy of job classes and grades and then fitting each job into a specific class and grade based on the opinions of unit supervisors

47. The above passage states that the system of classifying jobs MOST used in an organization is to

47.____

    A. organize all jobs in the organization in accordance with their requirements and then create categories or clusters of jobs
    B. classify all jobs in the organization according to the titles and rank by which they are currently known in the organization
    C. establish a pre-arranged series of grades or zones and then fit all jobs into one of the grades or zones
    D. determine the salary currently being paid for each job and then rank the jobs in order according to salary

48. According to the above passage, experience has shown that when a group of raters is assigned to the job evaluation task and each individual rates independently of the others, the raters GENERALLY

48.____

    A. agree with respect to all aspects of their rankings
    B. disagree with respect to all or nearly all aspects of the rankings
    C. disagree on overall ratings but agree on specific rating factors
    D. agree on overall ratings but have some variance in some details

49. The above paragraphs state that the use of a detailed job description is of special value   49.____
when

    A. employees of an organization have participated in the preliminary steps involved in actual preparation of the job description
    B. labor representatives are not participating in ranking of the jobs
    C. an individual rater who is unsure of himself is ranking the jobs
    D. a group of raters is having difficulty reaching unanimity with respect to ranking a certain job

50. A comparison of the various rating systems, as described in the above passage, shows   50.____
that

    A. the ranking system is not as appropriate for general use as a properly validated point system
    B. the point system is the same as the Factor Comparison Plan except that it places greater emphasis on money
    C. no system is capable of combining the point system and the Factor Comparison Plan
    D. the point system will be discontinued last when used in connection with the Factor Comparison Plan

---

KEY (CORRECT ANSWERS)

1.	B	11.	A	21.	C	31.	C	41.	C
2.	A	12.	B	22.	C	32.	D	42.	C
3.	C	13.	C	23.	A	33.	A	43.	B
4.	B	14.	C	24.	B	34.	A	44.	D
5.	D	15.	B	25.	C	35.	B	45.	B
6.	D	16.	C	26.	D	36.	B	46.	C
7.	A	17.	D	27.	B	37.	D	47.	A
8.	A	18.	D	28.	A	38.	B	48.	D
9.	B	19.	B	29.	B	39.	B	49.	D
10.	D	20.	A	30.	D	40.	D	50.	A

EXAMINATION SECTION

TEST 1

DIRECTIONS: Each question or incomplete statement is followed by several suggested answers or completions. Select the one that BEST answers the question or completes the statement. *PRINT THE LETTER OF THE CORRECT ANSWER IN THE SPACE AT THE RIGHT.*

1. A matriculated student at the City University of New York may BEST be described as one who
   A. is allowed a maximum credit load of 12 credits
   B. has paid full tuition
   C. has been admitted to the City University conditionally
   D. is enrolled in a program leading to a degree

   1._____

2. The Administrative Council of the City University of New York consists of the
   A. presidents of the University colleges
   B. vice-presidents of the University colleges
   C. directors of divisions of the University colleges
   D. deans of administration of the University colleges

   2._____

3. Of the following, the statement which BEST describes the policy of open admissions at the City University of New York is that
   A. any resident of New York City may visit and participate at any time in any classes offered by the City University
   B. all recent graduates of New York City high schools are eligible for admission to a college of the City University
   C. any adult is eligible for admission to the City University regardless of his educational background
   D. minority group members are assured of admission regardless of educational background

   3._____

4. Of the following degrees, the one which the community colleges of the City University of New York GENERALLY have the authority to grant is the
   A. master's degree   B. bachelor's degree
   C. specialist's degree   D. associate's degree

   4._____

5. Normally, a prospective student who is the holder of a New York State high school equivalency diploma
   A. is generally eligible for admission to undergraduate units of the City University
   B. will need to present a high school certificate as well as the equivalency diploma for admission to the City University
   C. is eligible for admission only to non-transfer programs of the community college units
   D. will need to qualify for admission by enrolling in an evening division program as a special student

   5._____

6. The FIRST terminal degree given by graduate schools *normally* is a
   - A. doctor's degree
   - B. associate's degree
   - C. specialist's degree
   - D. master's degree

6._____

7. Generally, non-matriculated students at the City University of New York would MOST frequently be enrolled in
   - A. evening sessions
   - B. day sessions
   - C. a graduate division
   - D. a Liberal Arts College

7._____

8. The City University of New York is an educational institution consisting of
   - A. all public and private colleges located in New York City
   - B. only the community colleges located in the five boroughs of New York City
   - C. the municipal college system of New York City
   - D. the graduate and professional schools financed in part by the City of New York

8._____

9. An employment officer seeking to recruit prospective medical laboratory technicians from the City University of New York should recruit PRIMARILY in
   - A. schools of education
   - B. university doctoral programs
   - C. community colleges
   - D. liberal arts programs

9._____

10. The CHIEF educational and administrative officer of the City University of New York as a whole is called the
    - A. Chancellor
    - B. President
    - C. Vice Chairman of the Board
    - D. University Dean

10._____

KEY (CORRECT ANSWERS)

1. D	6. D
2. A	7. A
3. B	8. C
4. D	9. C
5. A	10. A

EXAMINATION SECTION
TEST 1

DIRECTIONS: Each question or incomplete statement is followed by several suggested answers or completions. Select the one that BEST answers the question or completes the statement. *PRINT THE LETTER OF THE CORRECT ANSWER IN THE SPACE AT THE RIGHT.*

1. A supervisor notices that one of his more competent subordinates has recently been showing less interest in his work. The work performed by this employee has also fallen off and he seems to want to do no more than the minimum acceptable amount of work. When his supervisor questions the subordinate about his decreased interest and his mediocre work performance, the subordinate replies: *Sure, I've lost interest in my work. I don't see any reason why I should do more than I have to. When I do a good job, nobody notices it. But, let me fall down on one minor job and the whole place knows about it! So why should I put myself out on this job?*
   If the subordinate's contentions are true, it would be correct to assume that the

   A. subordinate has not received adequate training
   B. subordinate's workload should be decreased
   C. supervisor must share responsibility for this employee's reaction
   D. supervisor has not been properly enforcing work standards

1.____

2. *How many subordinates should report directly to each supervisor? While there is agreement that there are limits to the number of subordinates that a manager can supervise well, this limit is determined by a number of important factors.*
   Which of the following factors is most likely to increase the number of subordinates that can be effectively supervised by one supervisor in a particular unit?

   A. The unit has a great variety of activities
   B. A staff assistant handles the supervisor's routine duties
   C. The unit has a relatively inexperienced staff
   D. The office layout is being rearranged to make room for more employees

2.____

3. Mary Smith, an Administrative Assistant, heads the Inspection Records Unit of Department Y. She is a dedicated supervisor who not only strives to maintain an efficient operation, but she also tries to improve the competence of each individual member of her staff. She keeps these considerations in mind when assigning work to her staff. Her bureau chief asks her to compile some data based on information contained in her records. She feels that any member of her staff should be able to do this job. The one of the following members of her staff who would probably be given LEAST consideration for this assignment is

   A. Jane Abel, a capable Supervising Clerk with considerable experience in the unit
   B. Kenneth Brown, a Senior Clerk recently transferred to the unit who has not had an opportunity to demonstrate his capabilities
   C. Laura Chance, a Clerk who spends full time on a single routine assignment
   D. Michael Dunn, a Clerk who works on several minor jobs but still has the lightest workload

3.____

4. *There are very few aspects of a supervisor's job that do not involve communication, either in writing or orally.*
   Which of the following statements regarding oral and written orders is NOT correct?

4.____

A. Oral orders usually permit more immediate feedback than do written orders.
B. Written orders, rather than oral orders, should generally be given when the subordinate will be held strictly accountable.
C. Oral orders are usually preferable when the order contains lengthy detailed instructions.
D. Written orders, rather than oral orders, should usually be given to a subordinate who is slow to understand or is forgetful.

5. Assume that you are the head of a large clerical unit in Department R. Your department's personnel office has appointed a Clerk, Roberta Rowe, to fill a vacancy in your unit. Before bringing this appointee to your office, the personnel office has given Roberta the standard orientation on salary, fringe benefits, working conditions, attendance and the department's personnel rules. In addition, he has supplied her with literature covering these areas. Of the following, the action that you should take FIRST after Roberta has been brought to your office is to   5.____

   A. give her an opportunity to read the literature furnished by the personnel office so that she can ask you questions about it
   B. escort her to the desk she will use and assign her to work with an experienced employee who will act as her trainer
   C. explain the duties and responsibilities of her job and its relationship with the jobs being performed by the other employees of the unit
   D. summon the employee who is currently doing the work that will be performed by Roberta and have him explain and demonstrate how to perform the required tasks

6. Your superior informs you that the employee turnover rate in your office is well above the norm and must be reduced. Which one of the following initial steps would be LEAST appropriate in attempting to overcome this problem?   6.____

   A. Decide to be more lenient about performance standards and about employee requests for time off, so that your office will gain a reputation as an easy place to work
   B. Discuss the problem with a few of your key people whose judgment you trust to see if they can shed some light on the underlying causes of the problem
   C. Review the records of employees who have left during the past year to see if there is a pattern that will help you understand the problem
   D. Carefully review your training procedures to see whether they can be improved

7. In issuing instructions to a subordinate on a job assignment, the supervisor should ordinarily explain why the assignment is being made. Omission of such an explanation is best justified when the   7.____

   A. subordinate is restricted in the amount of discretion he can exercise in carrying out the assignment
   B. assignment is one that will be unpopular with the subordinate
   C. subordinate understands the reason as a result of previous similar assignments
   D. assignment is given to an employee who is in need of further training

8. When a supervisor allows sufficient time for training and makes an appropriate effort in the training of his subordinates, his chief goal is to   8.____

A. increase the dependence of one subordinate upon another in their everyday work activities
B. spend more time with his subordinates in order to become more involved in their work
C. increase the capability and independence of his subordinates in carrying out their work
D. increase his frequency of contact with his subordinates in order to better evaluate their performance

9. In preparing an evaluation of a subordinate's performance, which one of the following items is usually irrelevant?   9.____

    A. Remarks about tardiness or absenteeism
    B. Mention of any unusual contributions or accomplishments
    C. A summary of the employee's previous job experience
    D. An assessment of the employee's attitude toward the job

10. The ability to delegate responsibility while maintaining adequate controls is one key to a supervisor's success. Which one of the following methods of control would minimize the amount of responsibility assumed by the subordinate?   10.____

    A. Asking for a monthly status report in writing
    B. Asking to receive copies of important correspondence so that you can be aware of potential problems
    C. Scheduling periodic project status conferences with your subordinate
    D. Requiring that your subordinate confer with you before making decisions on a project

11. You wish to assign an important project to a subordinate who you think has good potential. Which one of the following approaches would be most effective in successfully completing the project while developing the subordinate's abilities?   11.____

    A. Describe the project to the subordinate in general terms and emphasize that it must be completed as quickly as possible
    B. Outline the project in detail to the subordinate and emphasize that its successful completion could lead to career advancement
    C. Develop a detailed project outline and timetable, discuss the details and timing with him and assign the subordinate to carry out the plan on his own
    D. Discuss the project objectives and suggested approaches with the subordinate, and ask the subordinate to develop a detailed project outline and timetable of your approval

12. Research studies reveal that an important difference between high-production and low-production supervisors lies not in their interest in eliminating mistakes, but in their manner of handling mistakes. High-production supervisors are most likely to look upon mistakes as primarily   12.____

    A. an opportunity to provide training
    B. a byproduct of subordinate negligence
    C. an opportunity to fix blame in a situation
    D. a result of their own incompetence

13. Supervisors should try to establish what has been called *positive discipline*, an atmo-   13.____
sphere in which subordinates willingly abide by rules which they consider fair. When a
supervisor notices a subordinate violating an important rule, his FIRST course of action
should be to

    A. stop the subordinate and tell him what he is doing wrong
    B. wait a day or two before approaching the employee involved
    C. call a meeting of all subordinates to discuss the rule
    D. forget the matter in the hope that it will not happen again

14. The working climate is the feeling, degree of freedom, the tone and the mood of the   14.____
working environment. Which of the following contributes most to determining the working
climate in a unit or group?

    A. The rules set for rest periods
    B. The example set by the supervisor
    C. The rules set for morning check-in
    D. The wages paid to the employees

15. John Polk is a bright, ingenious clerk with a lot of initiative. He has made many good sug-   15.____
gestions to his supervisor in the Training Division of Department T, where he is
employed. However, last week one of his bright ideas literally *blew up.* In setting up some
electronic equipment in the training classroom, he crossed some wires resulting in a
damaged tape recorder and a classroom so filled with smoke that the training class had
to be held in another room. When Mr. Brown, his supervisor, learned of this occurrence,
he immediately summoned John to his private office. There Mr. Brown spent five minutes
bawling John out, calling him an overzealous, overgrown kid, and sent him back to his job
without letting John speak once. Of the following, the action of Mr. Brown that most
deserves approval is that he

    A. took disciplinary action immediately without regard for past performance
    B. kept the disciplinary interview to a brief period
    C. concentrated his criticism on the root cause of the occurrence
    D. held the disciplinary interview in his private office .

16. Typically, when the technique of *supervision by results* is practiced, higher management   16.____
sets down, either implicitly or explicitly, certain performance standards or goals that the
subordinate is expected to meet. So long as these standards are met, management
interferes very little. The most likely result of the use of this technique is that it will

    A. lead to ambiguity in terms of goals
    B. be successful only to the extent that close direct supervision is practiced
    C. make it possible to evaluate both employee and supervisory effectiveness
    D. allow for complete autonomy on the subordinate's part

17. Assume that you, an Administrative Assistant, are the supervisor of a large clerical unit   17.____
performing routine clerical operations. One of your clerks consistently produces much
less work than other members of your staff performing similar tasks. Of the following, the
action you should take FIRST is to

    A. ask the clerk if he wants to be transferred to another unit

B. reprimand the clerk for his poor performance and warn him that further disciplinary action will be taken if his work does not improve
C. quietly ask the clerk's co-workers whether they know why his performance is poor
D. discuss this matter with the clerk to work out plans for improving his performance

18. When making written evaluations and reviews of the performance of subordinates, it is usually advisable to

18.____

A. avoid informing the employee of the evaluation if it is critical because it may create hard feelings
B. avoid informing the employee of the evaluation whether critical or favorable because it is tension-producing
C. permit the employee to see the evaluation but not to discuss it with him because the supervisor cannot be certain where the discussion might lead
D. discuss the evaluation openly with the employee because it helps the employee understand what is expected of him

19. There are a number of well-known and respected human relations principles that successful supervisors have been using for years in building good relationships with their employees. Which of the following does NOT illustrate such a principle?

19.____

A. Give clear and complete instructions
B. Let each person know how he is getting along
C. Keep an open-door policy
D. Make all relationships personal ones

20. Assume that it is your responsibility as an Administrative Assistant to maintain certain personnel records that are continually being updated. You have three senior clerks assigned specifically to this task. Recently you have noticed that the volume of work has increased substantially, and the processing of personnel records by the clerks is back-logged. Your supervisor is now receiving complaints due to the processing delay. Of the following, the best course of action for you to take FIRST is to

20.____

A. have a meeting with the clerks, advise them of the problem, and ask that they do their work faster; then confirm your meeting in writing for the record
B. request that an additional position be authorized for your unit
C. review the procedures being used for processing the work, and try to determine if you can improve the flow of work
D. get the system moving faster by spending some of your own time processing the backlog

21. Assume that you are in charge of a payroll unit consisting of four clerks. It is Friday, November 14. You have just arrived in the office after a conference. Your staff is preparing a payroll that must be forwarded the following Monday. Which of the following new items on your desk should you attend to FIRST?

21.____

A. A telephone message regarding very important information needed for the statistical summary of salaries paid for the month of November
B. A memorandum regarding a new procedure that should be followed in preparing the payroll
C. A telephone message from an employee who is threatening to endorse his pay-check *Under Protest* because he is dissatisfied with the amount

D.   A memorandum from your supervisor reminding you to submit the probationary period report on a new employee

22.   You are an Administrative Assistant in charge of a unit that orders and issues supplies. On a particular day you are faced with the following four situations. Which one should you take care of FIRST?   22.____

    A.   One of your employees who is in the process of taking the quarterly inventory of supplies has telephoned and asked that you return his call as soon as possible
    B.   A representative of a company that is noted for producing excellent office supplies will soon arrive with samples for you to distribute to the various offices in your agency
    C.   A large order of supplies which was delivered this morning has been checked and counted and a deliveryman is waiting for you to sign the receipt
    D.   A clerk from the purchase division asks you to search for a bill you failed to send to them which is urgently needed in order for them to complete a report due this morning

23.   As an Administrative Assistant, assume that it is necessary for you to give an unpleasant assignment to one of your subordinates. You expect this employee to raise some objections to this assignment. The most appropriate of the following actions for you to take FIRST is to issue the assignment   23.____

    A.   orally, with the further statement that you will not listen to any complaints
    B.   in writing, to forestall any complaints by the employee
    C.   orally, permitting the employee to express his feelings
    D.   in writing, with a note that any comments should be submitted in writing

24.   Assume that you are an Administrative Assistant supervising the Duplicating and Reproduction Unit of Department B. One of your responsibilities is to prepare a daily schedule showing when and on which of your unit's four duplicating machines jobs are to be run off. Of the following, the factor that should be given LEAST consideration in preparing the schedule is the   24.____

    A.   priority of each of the jobs to be run off
    B.   production speed of the different machines that will be used
    C.   staff available to operate the machines
    D.   date on which the job order was received

25.   *Cycling is an arrangement where papers are processed throughout a period according to an orderly plan rather than as a group all at one time. This technique has been used for a long time by public utilities in their cycle billing.* Of the following practices, the one that best illustrates this technique is that in which   25.____

    A.   paychecks for per annum employees are issued bi-weekly and those for per diem employees are issued weekly
    B.   field inspectors report in person to their offices one day a week, on Fridays, when they do all their paperwork and also pick up their paychecks
    C.   the dates for issuing relief checks to clients vary depending on the last digit of the clients' social security numbers
    D.   the last day for filing and paying income taxes is the same for Federal, State and City income taxes

26. The employees in your division have recently been given an excellent up-to-date office 26.____
manual, but you find that a good number of employees are not following the procedures
outlined in it. Which one of the following would be most likely to ensure that employees
begin using the manual effectively?

    A. Require each employee to keep a copy of the manual in plain sight on his desk
    B. Issue warnings periodically to those employees who deviate most from procedures
       prescribed in the manual
    C. Tell an employee to check his manual when he does not follow the proper proce-
       dures
    D. Suggest to the employees that the manual be studied thoroughly

27. The one of the following factors which should be considered FIRST in the design of office 27.____
forms is the

    A. information to be included in the form
    B. sequence of the information
    C. purpose of the form
    D. persons who will be using the form

28. *Window envelopes are being used to an increasing extent by government and private* 28.____
industry. The one of the following that is NOT an advantage of window envelopes is that
they

    A. cut down on addressing costs
    B. eliminate the need to attach envelopes to letters being sent forward for signature
       by a superior
    C. are less costly to buy than regular envelopes
    D. reduce the risk of having letters placed in wrong envelopes

29. Your bureau head asks you to prepare the office layouts for several of his units being 29.____
moved to a higher floor in your office building. Of the following possibilities, the one that
you should AVOID in preparing the layouts is to

    A. place the desks of the first-line supervisors near those of the staffs they supervise
    B. place the desks of employees whose work is most closely related near one another
    C. arrange the desks so that employees do not face one another
    D. locate desks with many outside visitors farthest from the office entrance

30. Which one of the following conditions would be LEAST important in considering a 30.____
change of the layout in a particular office?

    A. Installation of a new office machine
    B. Assignment of five additional employees to your office
    C. Poor flow of work
    D. Employees' personal preferences of desk location

31. Suppose Mr. Bloom, an Administrative Assistant, is dictating a letter to a stenographer. 31.____
His dictation begins with the name of the addressee and continues to the body of the letter. However, Mr. Bloom does not dictate the address of the recipient of the letter. He
expects the stenographer to locate it. The use of this practice by Mr. Bloom is

    A. acceptable, especially if he gives the stenographer the letter to which he is
       responding

    B.   acceptable, especially if the letter is lengthy and detailed
    C.   unacceptable, because it is not part of a stenographer's duties to search for information
    D.   unacceptable, because he should not rely on the accuracy of the stenographer

32.   Assume that there are no rules, directives or instructions concerning the filing of materials in your office or the retention of such files. A system is now being followed of placing in *inactive files any materials that are more than one year old. Of the following, the most appropriate thing to do with material that has been in an inactive* file in your office for more than one year is to   32._____

    A.   inspect the contents of the files to decide how to dispose of them
    B.   transfer the material to a remote location, where it can be obtained if necessary
    C.   keep the material intact for a minimum of another three years
    D.   destroy the material which has not been needed for at least a year

33.   Suppose you, an Administrative Assistant, have just returned to your desk after engaging in an all-morning conference. Joe Burns, a Clerk, informs you that Clara McClough, an administrator in another agency, telephoned during the morning and that, although she requested to speak with you, he was able to give her the desired information. Of the following, the most appropriate action for you to take in regard to Mr. Burns' action is to   33._____

    A.   thank him for assisting Ms. McClough in your absence
    B.   explain to him the proper telephone practice to use in the future
    C.   reprimand him for not properly channeling Ms. McClough's call
    D.   issue a memo to all clerical employees regarding proper telephone practices

34.   *When interviewing subordinates with problems, supervisors frequently find that asking direct questions of the employee results only in evasive responses. The supervisor may therefore resort to the non-directive interview technique. In this technique the supervisor avoids pointed questions; he leads the employee to continue talking freely uninfluenced by the supervisor's preconceived notions. This technique often enables the employee to bring his problem into sharp focus and to reach a solution to his problem.*   34._____
Suppose that you are a supervisor interviewing a subordinate about his recent poor attendance record. On calling his attention to his excessive lateness record, he replies: *I just don't seem to be able to get up in the morning. Frankly, I've lost interest in this job. I don't care about it. When I get up in the morning, I have to skip breakfast and I'm still late. I don't care about this job.*
If you are using the *non-directive* technique in this interview, the most appropriate of the following responses for you to make is

    A.   *You don't care about this job?*
    B.   *Don't you think you are letting your department down?*
    C.   *Are you having trouble at home?*
    D.   *Don't you realize your actions are childish?*

35.   An employee in a work group made the following comment to a co-worker: *It's great to be a lowly employee instead of an Administrative Assistant because you can work without thinking. The Administrative Assistant is getting paid to plan, schedule and think. Let him see to it that you have a productive day.*   35._____
Which one of the following statements about this quotation best reflects an understanding of good personnel management techniques and the role of the supervising Administrative Assistant?

A. The employee is wrong in attitude and in his perception of the role of the Administrative Assistant
B. The employee is correct in attitude but is wrong in his perception of the role of the Administrative Assistant
C. The employee is correct in attitude and in his perception of the role of the Administrative Assistant
D. The employee is wrong in attitude but is right in his perception of the role of the Administrative Assistant

—————

KEY (CORRECT ANSWERS)

1.	C	11.	D	26.	C
2.	B	12.	A	27.	C
3.	A	13.	A	28.	C
4.	C	14.	B	29.	D
5.	C	15.	D	30.	D
6.	A	16.	C/D	31.	A
7.	C	17.	D	32.	A/B
8.	C	18.	D	33.	A
9.	C	19.	D	34.	A
10.	D	20.	C	35.	D
		21.	B		
		22.	C		
		23.	C		
		24.	D		
		25.	C		

—————

TEST 2

DIRECTIONS: Each question or incomplete statement is followed by several suggested answers or completions. Select the one that BEST answers the question or completes the statement. *PRINT THE LETTER OF THE CORRECT ANSWER IN THE SPACE AT THE RIGHT.*

Questions 1 through 5 are to be answered solely on the basis of the following passage:

General supervision, in contrast to close supervision, involves a high degree of delegation of authority and requires some indirect means to ensure that employee behavior conforms to management needs. Not everyone works well under general supervision, however. General supervision works best where subordinates desire responsibility. General supervision also works well where individuals in work groups have strong feelings about the quality of the finished work products. Strong identification with management goals is another trait of persons who work well under general supervision. There are substantial differences in the amount of responsibility people are willing to accept on the job. One person may flourish under supervision that another might find extremely restrictive.

Psychological research provides evidence that the nature of a person's personality affects his attitude toward supervision. There are some employees with a low need for achievement and high fear of failure who shy away from challenges and responsibilities. Many seek self-expression off the job and ask only to be allowed to daydream on it. There are others who have become so accustomed to the authoritarian approach in their culture, family and previous work experience that they regard general supervision as no supervision at all. They abuse the privileges it bestows on them and refuse to accept the responsibilities it demands.

Different groups develop different attitudes toward work. Most college graduates, for example, expect a great deal of responsibility and freedom. People with limited education, on the other hand, often have trouble accepting the concept that people should make decisions for themselves, particularly decisions concerning work. Therefore, the extent to which general supervision will be effective varies greatly with the subordinates involved.

1. According to the above passage, which one of the following is a necessary part of management policy regarding general supervision?

    A. Most employees should formulate their own work goals
    B. Deserving employees should be rewarded periodically
    C. Some controls on employee work patterns should be established
    D. Responsibility among employees should generally be equalized

1.____

2. It can be inferred from the above passage that an employee who avoids responsibilities and challenges is most likely to

    A. gain independence under general supervision
    B. work better under close supervision than under general supervision
    C. abuse the liberal guidelines of general supervision
    D. become more restricted and cautious under general supervision

2.____

3. Based on the above passage, employees who succeed under general supervision are most likely to

    A. have a strong identification with people and their problems
    B. accept work obligations without fear
    C. seek self-expression off the job
    D. value the intellectual aspects of life

3.____

4. Of the following, the best title for the passage is 4.____

    A. Benefits and Disadvantages of General Supervision
    B. Production Levels of Employees Under General Supervision
    C. Employee Attitudes Toward Work and the Work Environment
    D. Employee Background and Personality as a Factor in Utilizing General Supervision

5. It can be inferred from the above passage that the one of the following employees who is most likely to work best under general supervision is one who 5.____

    A. is a part-time graduate student
    B. was raised by very strict parents
    C. has little self-confidence
    D. has been closely supervised in past jobs

Questions 6 through 10 are to be answered solely on the basis of the information in the following passage:

The concept of *program management* was first developed in order to handle some of the complex projects undertaken by the U.S. Department of Defense in the 1950's. Program management is an administrative system combining planning and control techniques to guide and coordinate all the activities which contribute to one overall program or project. It has been used by the federal government to manage space exploration and other programs involving many contributing organizations. It is also used by state and local governments and by some large firms to provide administrative integration of work from a number of sources, be they individuals, departments or outside companies.

One of the specific administrative techniques for program management is Program Evaluation Review Technique (PERT). PERT begins with the assembling of a list of all the activities needed to accomplish an overall task. The next step consists of arranging these activities in a sequential network showing both how much time each activity will take and which activities must be completed before others can begin. The time required for each activity is estimated by simple statistical techniques by the persons who will be responsible for the work, and the time required to complete the entire string of activities along each sequential path through the network is then calculated. There may be dozens or hundreds of these paths, so the calculation is usually done by computer. The longest path is then labeled the *critical path* because no matter how quickly events not on this path are completed, the events along the longest path must be finished before the project can be terminated. The overall starting and completion dates are then pinpointed, and target dates are established for each task. Actual progress can later be checked by comparison to the network plan.

6. Judging from the information in the above passage, which one of the following projects is most suitable for handling by a program management technique? 6.____

    A. Review and improvement of the filing system used by a city office
    B. Computerization of accounting data already on file in an office
    C. Planning and construction of an urban renewal project
    D. Announcing a change in city tax regulations to thousands of business firms

7. The passage indicates that program management methods are now in wide use by various kinds of organizations. Which one of the following organizations would you LEAST expect to make much use of such methods today? 7.____

A. An automobile manufacturer
B. A company in the aerospace business
C. The government of a large city
D. A library reference department

8. In making use of the PERT technique, the first step is to determine   8._____

A. every activity that must take place in order to complete the project
B. a target date for completion of the project
C. the estimated time required to complete each activity which is related to the whole
D. which activities will make up the longest path on the chart

9. Who estimates the time required to complete a particular activity in a PERT program?   9._____

A. The people responsible for the particular activity
B. The statistician assigned to the program
C. The organization that has commissioned the project
D. The operator who programs the computer

10. Which one of the following titles best describes the contents of the passage?   10._____

A. *The Need For Computers in Today's Projects*
B. *One Technique For Program Management*
C. *Local Governments Can Now Use Space-Age Techniques*
D. *Why Planning Is Necessary For Complex Projects*

11. An Administrative Assistant has been criticized for the low productivity in the group which   11._____
he supervises. Which of the following best reflects an understanding of supervisory
responsibilities in the area of productivity? An Administrative Assistant should be held
responsible for

A. his own individual productivity and the productivity of the group he supervises,
because he is in a position where he maintains or increases production through
others
B. his own personal productivity only, because the supervisor is not likely to have any
effect on the productivity of subordinates
C. his own individual productivity but only for a drop in the productivity of the group he
supervises, since subordinates will receive credit for increased productivity individually
D. his own personal productivity only, because this is how he would be evaluated if he
were not a supervisor

12. A supervisor has held a meeting in his office with an employee about the employee's   12._____
grievance. The grievance concerned the sharp way in which the supervisor reprimanded
the employee for an error the employee made in the performance of a task assigned to
him. The problem was not resolved. Which one of the following statements about this
meeting best reflects an understanding of good supervisory techniques?

A. It is awkward for a supervisor to handle a grievance involving himself. The supervisor should not have held the meeting.
B. It would have been better if the supervisor had held the meeting at the employee's
workplace, even though there would have been frequent distractions, because the
employee would have been more relaxed.

C. The resolution of a problem is not the only sign of a successful meeting. The achievement of communication was worthwhile.

D. The supervisor should have been forceful. There is nothing wrong with raising your voice to an employee every once in a while.

13. John Hayden, the owner of a single-family house, complains that he submitted an application for reduction of assessment that obviously was not acted upon before his final assessment notice was sent to him. The timely receipt of the application has been verified in a departmental log book. As the supervisor of the clerical unit through which this application was processed and where this delay occurred, you should be LEAST concerned with

13.____

A. what happened   B. who is responsible
C. why it happened   D. what can be learned from it

14. The one of the following that applies most appropriately to the role of the first-line supervisor is that usually he is

14.____

A. called upon to help determine agency policy
B. involved in long-range agency planning
C. responsible for determining some aspects of basic organization structure
D. a participant in developing procedures and methods

15. Sally Jones, an Administrative Assistant, gives clear and precise instructions to Robert Warren, a Senior Clerk. In these instructions, Ms. Jones clearly delegates authority to Mr. Warren to undertake a well-defined task. In this situation Ms. Jones should expect Mr. Warren to

15.____

A. come to her to check out details as he progresses with the task
B. come to her only with exceptional problems
C. ask her permission if he wishes to use his delegated authority
D. use his authority to redefine the task and its related activities

16. Planning involves establishing departmental goals and programs and determining ways of reaching them. The main advantage of such planning is that

16.____

A. there will be no need for adjustments once a plan is put into operation
B. it ensures that everyone is working on schedule
C. it provides the framework for an effective operation
D. unexpected work problems are easily overcome

17. As a result of reorganization, the jobs in a large clerical unit were broken down into highly specialized tasks. Each specialized task was then assigned to a particular employee to perform. This action will probably lead to an increase in

17.____

A. flexibility   B. job satisfaction
C. need for coordination   D. employee initiative

18. Your office carries on a large volume of correspondence concerned with the purchase of supplies and equipment for city offices. You use form letters to deal with many common situations. In which one of the following situations would use of a form letter be LEAST appropriate?

18.____

A. Informing suppliers of a change in city regulations concerning purchase contracts
B. Telling a new supplier the standard procedures to be followed in billing
C. Acknowledging receipt of a complaint and saying that the complaint will be investigated
D. Answering a city councilman's request for additional information on a particular regulation affecting suppliers

19. Assume that you are an Administrative Assistant heading a large clerical unit. Because of the great demands being made on your time, you have designated Tom Smith, a Supervising Clerk, to be your assistant and to assume some of your duties. Of the following duties performed by you, the most appropriate one to assign to Tom Smith is to

    19.____

A. conduct the on-the-job training of new employees
B. prepare the performance appraisal reports on your staff members
C. represent your unit in dealings with the heads of other units
D. handle matters that require exception to general policy

20. In establishing rules for his subordinates, a superior should be primarily concerned with

    20.____

A. creating sufficient flexibility to allow for exceptions
B. making employees aware of the reasons for the rules and the penalties for infractions
C. establishing the strength of his own position in relation to his subordinates
D. having his subordinates know that such rules will be imposed in a personal manner

21. The practice of conducting staff training sessions on a periodic basis is generally considered

    21.____

A. poor; it takes employees away from their work assignments
B. poor; all staff training should be done on an individual basis
C. good; it permits the regular introduction of new methods and techniques
D. good; it ensures a high employee productivity rate

22. Suppose, as an Administrative Assistant, you have just announced at a staff meeting with your subordinates that a radical reorganization of work will take place next week. Your subordinates at the meeting appear to be excited, tense and worried. Of the following, the best action for you to take at that time is to

    22.____

A. schedule private conferences with each subordinate to obtain his reaction to the meeting
B. close the meeting and tell your subordinates to return immediately to their work assignments
C. give your subordinates some time to ask questions and discuss your announcement
D. insist that your subordinates do not discuss your announcement among themselves or with other members of the agency

23. Suppose that as an Administrative Assistant you were recently placed in charge of the Duplicating and Stock Unit of Department Y. From your observation of the operations of your unit during your first week as its head, you get the impression that there are inefficiencies in its operations causing low productivity. To obtain an increase in its productivity, the FIRST of the following actions you should take is to

    23.____

A. seek the advice of your immediate superior on how he would tackle this problem
B. develop plans to correct any unsatisfactory conditions arising from other than man-power deficiencies
C. identify the problems causing low productivity
D. discuss your productivity problem with other unit heads to find out how they han-dled similar problems

24. Assume that you are an Administrative Assistant recently placed in charge of a large clerical unit. At a meeting, the head of another unit tells you, *My practice is to give a worker more than he can finish. In that way you can be sure that you are getting the most out of him.* For you to adopt this practice would be

    24.____

    A. advisable, since your actions would be consistent with those practiced in your agency
    B. inadvisable, since such a practice is apt to create frustration and lower staff morals
    C. advisable, since a high goal stimulates people to strive to attain it
    D. inadvisable, since management may, in turn, set too high a productivity goal for the unit

25. Suppose that you are the supervisor of a unit in which there is an increasing amount of friction among several of your staff members. One of the reasons for this friction is that the work of some of these staff members cannot be completed until other staff members complete related work. Of the following, the most appropriate action for you to take is to

    25.____

    A. summon these employees to a meeting to discuss the responsibilities each has and to devise better methods of coordination
    B. have a private talk with each employee involved and make each understand that there must be more cooperation among the employees
    C. arrange for interviews with each of the employees involved to determine what his problems are
    D. shift the assignments of these employees so that each will be doing a job different from his current one

26. An office supervisor has a number of responsibilities with regard to his subordinates. Which one of the following functions should NOT be regarded as a basic responsibility of the office supervisor?

    26.____

    A. Telling employees how to solve personal problems that may be interfering with their work
    B. Training new employees to do the work assigned to them
    C. Evaluating employees' performance periodically and discussing the evaluation with each employee
    D. Bringing employee grievances to the attention of higher-level administrators and seeking satisfactory resolutions

27. One of your most productive subordinates frequently demonstrates a poor attitude toward his job. He seems unsure of himself, and he annoys his co-workers because he is continually belittling himself and the work that he is doing. In trying to help him overcome this problem, which of the following approaches is LEAST likely to be effective?

    27.____

A. Compliment him on his work and assign him some additional responsibilities, telling him that he is being given these responsibilities because of his demonstrated ability

B. Discuss with him the problem of his attitude, and warn him that you will have to report it on his next performance evaluation

C. Assign him a particularly important and difficult project, stressing your confidence in his ability to complete it successfully

D. Discuss with him the problem of his attitude, and ask him for suggestions as to how you can help him overcome it

28. You come to realize that a personality conflict between you and one of your subordinates is adversely affecting his performance. Which one of the following would be the most appropriate FIRST step to take?   28._____

A. Report the problem to your superior and request assistance. His experience may be helpful in resolving this problem.

B. Discuss the situation with several of the subordinate's co-workers to see if they can suggest any remedy.

C. Suggest to the subordinate that he get professional counseling or therapy.

D. Discuss the situation candidly with the subordinate, with the objective of resolving the problem between yourselves.

29. Assume that you are an Administrative Assistant supervising the Payroll Records Section in Department G. Your section has been requested to prepare and submit to the department's budget officer a detailed report giving a breakdown of labor costs under various departmental programs and sub-programs. You have assigned this task to a Supervising Clerk, giving him full authority for seeing that this job is performed satisfactorily. You have given him a written statement of the job to be done and explained the purpose and use of this report. The next step that you should take in connection with this delegated task is to   29._____

A. assist the Supervising Clerk in the step-by-step performance of the job

B. assure the Supervising Clerk that you will be understanding of mistakes if made at the beginning

C. require him to receive your approval for interim reports submitted at key points before he can proceed further with his task

D. give him a target date for the completion of this report

30. Assume that you are an Administrative Assistant heading a unit staffed with six clerical employees. One Clerk, John Snell, is a probationary employee appointed four months ago. During the first three months, John learned his job quickly, performed his work accurately and diligently, and was cooperative and enthusiastic in his attitude. However, during the past few weeks his enthusiasm seems dampened, he is beginning to make mistakes and at times appears bored. Of the following, the most appropriate action for you to take is to   30._____

A. check with John's co-workers to find out whether they can explain John's change in attitude and work habits

B. wait a few more weeks before taking any action, so that John will have an opportunity to make the needed changes on his own initiative

C. talk to John about the change in his work performance and his decreased enthusiasm

D.   change John's assignment since this may be the basic cause of John's change in attitude and performance

31. The supervisor of a clerical unit, on returning from a meeting, finds that one of his subor-   31._____
     dinates is performing work not assigned by him. The subordinate explains that the group
     supervisor had come into the office while the unit supervisor was out and directed the
     employee to work on an urgent assignment. This is the first time the group supervisor
     had bypassed the unit supervisor. Of the following, the most appropriate action for the
     unit supervisor to take is to

     A.   explain to the group supervisor that bypassing the unit supervisor is an undesirable
          practice
     B.   have the subordinate stop work on the assignment until the entire matter can be
          clarified with the group supervisor
     C.   raise the matter of bypassing a supervisor at the next staff conference held by the
          group supervisor
     D.   forget about the incident

32. Assume that you are an Administrative Assistant in charge of the Mail and Records Unit   32._____
     of Department K. On returning from a meeting, you notice that Jane Smith is not at her
     regular work location. You learn that another employee, Ruth Reed, had become faint,
     and that Jane took Ruth outdoors for some fresh air. It is a long-standing rule in your unit
     that no employee is to leave the building during office hours except on official business or
     with the unit head's approval. Only a few weeks ago, John Duncan was reprimanded by
     you for going out at 10:00 a.m. for a cup of coffee. With respect to Jane Smith's violation
     of this rule, the most appropriate of the following actions for you to take is to

     A.   issue a reprimand to Jane Smith, with an explanation that all employees must be
          treated in exactly the same way
     B.   tell Jane that you should reprimand her, but you will not do so in this instance
     C.   overlook this rule violation in view of the extenuating circumstances
     D.   issue the reprimand with no further explanation, treating her in the same manner
          that you treated John Duncan

33. Assume that you are an Administrative Assistant recently assigned as supervisor of   33._____
     Department X's Mail and Special Services Unit. In addition to processing your depart-
     ment's mail, your clerical employees are often sent on errands in the city. You have
     learned that, while on such official errands, these clerks sometimes take care of their
     own personal matters or those of their co-workers. The previous supervisor had tolerated
     this practice even though it violated a departmental personnel rule. The most appropriate
     of the following actions for you to take is to

     A.   continue to tolerate this practice so long as it does not interfere with the work of
          your unit
     B.   take no action until you have proof that an employee has violated this rule; then
          give a mild reprimand
     C.   wait until an employee has committed a gross violation of this rule; then bring him
          up on charges
     D.   discuss this rule with your staff and caution them that its violation might necessitate
          disciplinary action

34. *Supervisors who exercise 'close supervision' over their subordinates usually check up on their employees frequently, give them frequent instructions and, in general, limit their freedom to do their work in their own way. Those who exercise 'general supervision' usually set forth the objectives of a job, tell their subordinates what they want accomplished, fix the limits within which the subordinates can work and let the employees (if they are capable) decide how the job is to be done.* Which one of the following conditions would contribute LEAST to the success of the *general supervision* approach in an organizational unit?

    A.   Employees in the unit welcome increased responsibilities
    B.   Work assignments in the unit are often challenging
    C.   Work procedures must conform with those of other units
    D.   Staff members support the objectives of the unit

34._____

35. Assume that you are an Administrative Assistant assigned as supervisor of the Clerical Services Unit of a large agency's Labor Relations Division. A member of your staff comes to you with a criticism of a policy followed by the Labor Relations Division. You also have similar views regarding this policy. Of the following, the most appropriate action for you to take in response to his criticism is to

    A.   agree with him, but tell him that nothing can be done about it at your level
    B.   suggest to him that it is not wise for him to express criticism of policy
    C.   tell the employee that he should direct his criticism to the head of your agency if he wants quick action
    D.   ask the employee if he has suggestions for revising the policy

35._____

KEY (CORRECT ANSWERS)

1.	C	11.	A	26.	A
2.	B	12.	C	27.	B
3.	B	13.	B	28.	D
4.	D	14.	D	29.	D
5.	A	15.	B	30.	C
6.	C	16.	C	31.	D
7.	D	17.	C	32.	C
8.	A	18.	D	33.	D
9.	A	19.	A	34.	C
10.	B	20.	B	35.	D
		21.	C		
		22.	C		
		23.	C		
		24.	B		
		25.	A		

TEST 3

DIRECTIONS: Each question or incomplete statement is followed by several suggested answers or completions. Select the one that BEST answers the question or completes the statement. *PRINT THE LETTER OF THE CORRECT ANSWER IN THE SPACE AT THE RIGHT.*

1. At the request of your bureau head you have designed a simple visitor's referral form. The form will be cut from 8-1/2" x 11" stock.
   Which of the following should be the dimensions of the form if you want to be sure that there is no waste of paper?

   A. 2-3/4" x 4-1/4"   B. 3-1/4" x 4-3/4"
   C. 3-3/4" x 4-3/4"   D. 4-1/2" x 5-1/2"

1.____

2. An office contains six file cabinets, each containing three drawers. One of your responsibilities as a new Administrative Assistant is to see that there is sufficient filing space. At the present time, 1/4 of the file space contains forms, 2/9 contains personnel records, 1/3 contains reports, and 1/7 of the remaining space contains budget records.
   If each drawer may contain more than one type of record, how much drawer space is now *empty*?

   A. 0 drawers   B. 13/14 of a drawer
   C. 3 drawers   D. 3-1/2 drawers

2.____

3. Assume that there were 21 working days in March. The five clerks in your unit had the following number of absences in March:
   Clerk H - 2 absences
   Clerk J - 1 absence
   Clerk K - 6 absences
   Clerk L - 0 absences
   Clerk M - 10 absences

   To the nearest day, what was the *average* attendance in March for the five clerks in your unit?

   A. 4   B. 17   C. 18   D. 21

3.____

Questions 4-12

DIRECTIONS: Questions 4 through 12 each consist of a sentence which may or may not be an example of good English usage. Consider grammar, punctuation, spelling, capitalization, verbosity, awkwardness, etc. Examine each sentence, and then choose the correct statement about it from the four choices below it. If the English usage in the sentence is better as given than with any of the changes suggested in options B, C or D, choose option A.

4. The stenographers who are secretaries to commissioners have more varied duties than the stenographic pool.

   A. This is an example of effective writing.
   B. In this sentence there would be a comma after *commissioners* in order to break up the sentence into clauses.
   C. In this sentence the words *stenographers in* should be inserted after the word *than*.
   D. In this sentence the word *commissioners* is misspelled.

4.____

5. A person who becomes an administrative assistant will be called upon to provide leader-ship, to insure proper quantity and quality of production, and many administrative chores must be performed.

    A. This sentence is an example of effective writing.
    B. The sentence should be divided into three separate sentences, each describing a duty.
    C. The words *many administrative chores must be performed* should be changed to *to perform many administrative chores.*
    D. The words *to provide leadership* should be changed to *to be a leader.*

5.____

6. A complete report has been submitted by our branch office, giving details about this transaction.

    A. This sentence is an example of effective writing.
    B. The phrase *giving details about this transaction* should be placed between the words *report* and *has.*
    C. A semi-colon should replace the comma after the word *office* to indicate indepen-dent clauses.
    D. A colon should replace the comma after the word *office* since the second clause provides further explanation.

6.____

7. The report was delayed because of the fact that the writer lost his rough draft two days before the deadline.

    A. This sentence is an example of effective writing.
    B. In this sentence the words *of the fact that* are unnecessary and should be deleted.
    C. In this sentence the words *because of the fact that* should be shortened to *due to.*
    D. In this sentence the word *before* should be replaced by *prior to.*

7.____

8. Included in this offer are a six months' guarantee, a complete set of instructions, and one free inspection of the equipment.

    A. This sentence is an example of effective writing.
    B. The word *is* should be substituted for the word *are.*
    C. The word *months* should have been spelled *month's.*
    D. The word *months* should be spelled *months.*

8.____

9. Certain employees come to the attention of their employers. Especially those with poor work records and excessive absences.

    A. This sentence is an example of effective writing.
    B. The period after the word *employers* should be changed to a comma, and the first letter of the word *Especially* should be changed to a small *e.*
    C. The period after the word *employers* should be changed to a semicolon, and the first letter of the word *Especially* should be changed to a small *e.*
    D. The period after the word *employers* should be changed to a colon.

9.____

10. The applicant had decided to decline the appointment by the time he was called for the interview.

10.____

A. This sentence is an example of effective writing.
B. In this sentence the word *had* should be deleted.
C. In this sentence the phrase *was called* should be replaced by *had been called*.
D. In this sentence the phrase *had decided to decline* should be replaced by *declined*.

11. There are two elevaters, each accommodating ten people.　　　　　　11.____

    A. This sentence is correct.
    B. In this sentence the word *elevaters* should be spelled *elevators*.
    C. In this sentence the word *each* should be replaced by the word *both*.
    D. In this sentence the word *accommodating* should be spelled *accomodating*.

12. With the aid of a special device, it was possible to alter the letterhead on the depart-　　12.____
ment's stationary.

    A. This sentence is correct.
    B. The word *aid* should be spelled *aide*.
    C. The word *device* should be spelled *devise*.
    D. The word *stationary* should be spelled *stationery*.

13. Examine the following sentence and then choose from the options below the correct　　13.____
word to be inserted in the blank space.
Everybody in both offices _____ involved in the project.

    A. are   B. feel   C. is

Questions 14-18

DIRECTIONS:　Answer questions 14 through 18 SOLELY on the basis of the information in the following passage.

A new way of looking at job performance promises to be a major advance in measuring and increasing a person's true effectiveness in business. The fact that individuals differ enormously in their judgment of when a piece of work is actually finished is significant. It is believed that more than half of all people in the business world are defective in the *sense of closure*, that is they do not know the proper time to throw the switch that turns off their effort in one direction and diverts it to a new job. Only a minority of workers at any level have the required judgment and the feeling of responsibility to work on a job to the point of maximum effectiveness. The vast majority let go of each task far short of the completion point.

Very often, a defective sense of closure exists in an entire staff. When that occurs, it usually stems from a long-standing laxness on the part of higher management. A low degree of responsibility has been accepted and it has come to be standard. Combating this requires implementation of a few basic policies. Firstly, it is important to make each responsibility completely clear and to set certain guideposts as to what constitutes complete performance. Secondly, excuses for delays and failures should not be dealt with too sympathetically, but interest should be shown in the encountered obstacles. Lastly, a checklist should be used periodically to determine whether new levels of expectancy and new closure values have been set.

14. According to the above passage, a *majority of* people in the business world　　14.____

    A. do not complete their work on time

    B.   cannot properly determine when a particular job is completed
    C.   make lame excuses for not completing a job on time
    D.   can adequately judge their own effectiveness at work

15.   It can be *inferred from* the above passage that when a poor sense of closure is observed   15.____
    among all the employees in a unit, the responsibility for raising the performance level
    belongs to

    A.   non-supervisory employees
    B.   the staff as a whole
    C.   management
    D.   first-line supervisors

16.   It is *implied by* the above passage that, by the establishment of work guideposts, employ-   16.____
    ees may develop a

    A.   better understanding of expected performances
    B.   greater interest in their work relationships
    C.   defective sense of closure
    D.   lower level of performance

17.   It can be inferred from the above passage that an individual's idea of whether a job is fin-   17.____
    ished is *most closely* associated with his

    A.   loyalty to management
    B.   desire to overcome obstacles
    C.   ability to recognize his own defects
    D.   sense of responsibility

18.   Of the following, the BEST heading for the above passage is   18.____

    A.   Management's Role in a Large Bureaucracy
    B.   Knowing When a Job is Finished
    C.   The Checklist, a Supervisor's Tool for Effectiveness
    D.   Supervisory Techniques

Questions 19-25

DIRECTIONS: Answer questions 19 through 25 assuming that you are in charge of public
                information for an office which issues reports and answers questions from
                other offices and from the public on changes in land use. The charts below
                represent comparative land use in four neighborhoods. The area of each
                neighborhood is expressed in city blocks. Assume that all city blocks are the
                same size.

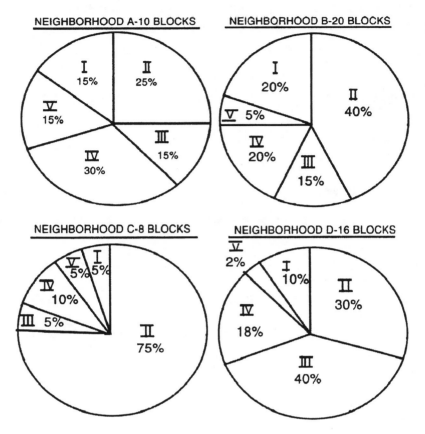

KEY: I - One- and two-family houses
      II - Apartment buildings
      III - Office buildings
      IV - Retail stores
      V - Factories and warehouses

19. In how many of these neighborhoods does residential use (categories I and II together)   19.____
    account for *more than 50%* of the land use?

    A. 1   B. 2   C. 3   D. 4

20. How many of the neighborhoods have an area of land occupied by apartment buildings   20.____
    which is *greater than* the area of land occupied by apartment buildings in Neighborhood
    C?

    A. none   B. 1   C. 2   D. 3

21. Which neighborhood has the LARGEST land area occupied by factories and ware-   21.____
    houses?

    A. A   B. B   C. C   D. D

22. In which neighborhood is the LARGEST percentage of the land devoted to *both* office   22.____
    buildings and retail stores?

    A. A   B. B   C. C   D. D

23. What is the difference, to the nearest city block, between the amount of land devoted to one- and two-family houses in Neighborhood A and the amount devoted to similar use in Neighborhood C?   23._____

    A. 1 block   B. 2 blocks   C. 5 blocks   D. 10 blocks

24. Which one of the following types of buildings occupies the same amount of land area in Neighborhood B as the amount of land area occupied by retail stores in Neighborhood A?   24._____

    A. Apartment buildings
    B. Office buildings
    C. Retail stores
    D. Factories and warehouses

25. Based on the information in the charts, which one of the following statements must be TRUE?   25._____

    A. Factories and warehouses are gradually disappearing from all the neighborhoods except Neighborhood A.
    B. Neighborhood B has more land area occupied by retail stores than any of the other neighborhoods.
    C. There are more apartment dwellers living in Neighborhood C than in any of the other neighborhoods.
    D. All four of these neighborhoods are predominantly residential.

_____

KEY (CORRECT ANSWERS)

1.	A		11.	B
2.	C		12.	D
3.	B		13.	C
4.	C		14.	B
5.	C		15.	C
6.	B		16.	A
7.	B		17.	D
8.	A		18.	B
9.	B		19.	B
10.	A		20.	B

21.	A
22.	D
23.	A
24.	B
25.	B

_____

PHILOSOPHY, PRINCIPLES, PRACTICES AND TECHNICS
OF
SUPERVISION, ADMINISTRATION, MANAGEMENT AND ORGANIZATION

TABLE OF CONTENTS

PHILOSOPHY, PRINCIPLES, PRACTICES, AND TECHNICS
OF
SUPERVISION, ADMINISTRATION, MANAGEMENT AND ORGANIZATION

I. MEANING OF SUPERVISION

The extension of the democratic philosophy has been accompanied by an extension in the scope of supervision. Modern leaders and supervisors no longer think of supervision in the narrow sense of being confined chiefly to visiting employees, supplying materials, or rating the staff. They regard supervision as being intimately related to all the concerned agencies of society, they speak of the supervisor's function in terms of "growth", rather than the "improvement," of employees.

This modern concept of supervision may be defined as follows:

Supervision is leadership and the development of leadership within groups which are cooperatively engaged in inspection, research, training, guidance and evaluation.

II. THE OLD AND THE NEW SUPERVISION

TRADITIONAL
1. Inspection
2. Focused on the employee
3. Visitation
4. Random and haphazard
5. Imposed and authoritarian
6. One person usually

MODERN
1. Study and analysis
2. Focused on aims, materials, methods, supervisors, employees, environment
3. Demonstrations, intervisitation, workshops, directed reading, bulletins, etc.
4. Definitely organized and planned (scientific)
5. Cooperative and democratic
6. Many persons involved (creative)

III THE EIGHT (8) BASIC PRINCIPLES OF THE NEW SUPERVISION

1. PRINCIPLE OF RESPONSIBILITY
Authority to act and responsibility for acting must be joined.
   a. If you give responsibility, give authority.
   b. Define employee duties clearly.
   c. Protect employees from criticism by others.
   d. Recognize the rights as well as obligations of employees.
   e. Achieve the aims of a democratic society insofar as it is possible within the area of your work.
   f. Establish a situation favorable to training and learning.
   g. Accept ultimate responsibility for everything done in your section, unit, office, division, department.
   h. Good administration and good supervision are inseparable.

2. *PRINCIPLE OF AUTHORITY*

The success of the supervisor is measured by the extent to which the power of authority is not used.

 a. Exercise simplicity and informality in supervision.
 b. Use the simplest machinery of supervision.
 c. If it is good for the organization as a whole, it is probably justified.
 d. Seldom be arbitrary or authoritative.
 e. Do not base your work on the power of position or of personality.
 f. Permit and encourage the free expression of opinions.

3. *PRINCIPLE OF SELF-GROWTH*

The success of the supervisor is measured by the extent to which, and the speed with which, he is no longer needed.

 a. Base criticism on principles, not on specifics.
 b. Point out higher activities to employees.
 c. Train for self-thinking by employees, to meet new situations.
 d. Stimulate initiative, self-reliance and individual responsibility.
 e. Concentrate on stimulating the growth of employees rather than on removing defects.

4. *PRINCIPLE OF INDIVIDUAL WORTH*

Respect for the individual is a paramount consideration in supervision.

 a. Be human and sympathetic in dealing with employees.
 b. Don't nag about things to be done.
 c. Recognize the individual differences among employees and seek opportunities to permit best expression of each personality.

5. *PRINCIPLE OF CREATIVE LEADERSHIP*

The best supervision is that which is not apparent to the employee.

 a. Stimulate, don't drive employees to creative action.
 b. Emphasize doing good things.
 c. Encourage employees to do what they do best.
 d. Do not be too greatly concerned with details of subject or method.
 e. Do not be concerned exclusively with immediate problems and activities.
 f. Reveal higher activities and make them both desired and maximally possible.
 g. Determine procedures in the light of each situation but see that these are derived from a sound basic philosophy.
 h. Aid, inspire and lead so as to liberate the creative spirit latent in all good employees.

6. *PRINCIPLE OF SUCCESS AND FAILURE*

There are no unsuccessful employees, only unsuccessful supervisors who have failed to give proper leadership.

 a. Adapt suggestions to the capacities, attitudes, and prejudices of employees.
 b. Be gradual, be progressive, be persistent.
 c. Help the employee find the general principle; have the employee apply his own problem to the general principle.
 d. Give adequate appreciation for good work and honest effort.
 e. Anticipate employee difficulties and help to prevent them.
 f. Encourage employees to do the desirable things they will do anyway.
 g. Judge your supervision by the results it secures.

7. PRINCIPLE OF SCIENCE
Successful supervision is scientific, objective, and experimental. It is based on facts, not on prejudices.
- a. Be cumulative in results.
- b. Never divorce your suggestions from the goals of training.
- c. Don't be impatient of results.
- d. Keep all matters on a professional, not a personal level.
- e. Do not be concerned exclusively with immediate problems and activities.
- f. Use objective means of determining achievement and rating where possible.

8. PRINCIPLE OF COOPERATION
Supervision is a cooperative enterprise between supervisor and employee.
- a. Begin with conditions as they are.
- b. Ask opinions of all involved when formulating policies.
- c. Organization is as good as its weakest link.
- d. Let employees help to determine policies and department programs.
- e. Be approachable and accessible - physically and mentally.
- f. Develop pleasant social relationships.

IV. WHAT IS ADMINISTRATION?

Administration is concerned with providing the environment, the material facilities, and the operational procedures that will promote the maximum growth and development of supervisors and employees. (Organization is an aspect, and a concomitant, of administration.)

There is no sharp line of demarcation between supervision and administration; these functions are intimately interrelated and, often, overlapping. They are complementary activities.

1. PRACTICES COMMONLY CLASSED AS "SUPERVISORY"
- a. Conducting employees conferences
- b. Visiting sections, units, offices, divisions, departments
- c. Arranging for demonstrations
- d. Examining plans
- e. Suggesting professional reading
- f. Interpreting bulletins
- g. Recommending in-service training courses
- h. Encouraging experimentation
- i. Appraising employee morale
- j. Providing for intervisitation

2. PRACTICES COMMONLY CLASSIFIED AS "ADMINISTRATIVE"
- a. Management of the office
- b. Arrangement of schedules for extra duties
- c. Assignment of rooms or areas
- d. Distribution of supplies
- e. Keeping records and reports
- f. Care of audio-visual materials
- g. Keeping inventory records
- h. Checking record cards and books
- i. Programming special activities
- j. Checking on the attendance and punctuality of employees

3. *PRACTICES COMMONLY CLASSIFIED AS BOTH "SUPERVISORY" AND "ADMINISTRATIVE"*
   a. Program construction
   b. Testing or evaluating outcomes
   c. Personnel accounting
   d. Ordering instructional materials

V. RESPONSIBILITIES OF THE SUPERVISOR

A person employed in a supervisory capacity must constantly be able to improve his own efficiency and ability. He represents the employer to the employees and only continuous self-examination can make him a capable supervisor.

Leadership and training are the supervisor's responsibility. An efficient working unit is one in which the employees work with the supervisor. It is his job to bring out the best in his employees. He must always be relaxed, courteous and calm in his association with his employees. Their feelings are important, and a harsh attitude does not develop the most efficient employees.

VI. COMPETENCIES OF THE SUPERVISOR

1. Complete knowledge of the duties and responsibilities of his position.
2. To be able to organize a job, plan ahead and carry through.
3. To have self-confidence and initiative.
4. To be able to handle the unexpected situation and make quick decisions.
5. To be able to properly train subordinates in the positions they are best suited for.
6. To be able to keep good human relations among his subordinates.
7. To be able to keep good human relations between his subordinates and himself and to earn their respect and trust.

VII. THE PROFESSIONAL SUPERVISOR-EMPLOYEE RELATIONSHIP

There are two kinds of efficiency: one kind is only apparent and is produced in organizations through the exercise of mere discipline; this is but a simulation of the second, or true, efficiency which springs from spontaneous cooperation. If you are a manager, no matter how great or small your responsibility, it is your job, in the final analysis, to create and develop this involuntary cooperation among the people whom you supervise. For, no matter how powerful a combination of money, machines, and materials a company may have, this is a dead and sterile thing without a team of willing, thinking and articulate people to guide it.

The following 21 points are presented as indicative of the exemplary basic relationship that should exist between supervisor and employee:

1. Each person wants to be liked and respected by his fellow employee and wants to be treated with consideration and respect by his superior.
2. The most competent employee will make an error. However, in a unit where good relations exist between the supervisor and his employees, tenseness and fear do not exist. Thus, errors are not hidden or covered up and the efficiency of a unit is not impaired.
3. Subordinates resent rules, regulations, or orders that are unreasonable or unexplained.
4. Subordinates are quick to resent unfairness, harshness, injustices and favoritism.
5. An employee will accept responsibility if he knows that he will be complimented for a job well done, and not too harshly chastised for failure; that his supervisor will check the cause of the failure, and, if it was the supervisor's fault, he will assume the blame therefore. If it was the employee's fault, his supervisor will explain the correct method or means of handling the responsibility.

6. An employee wants to receive credit for a suggestion he has made, that is used. If a suggestion cannot be used, the employee is entitled to an explanation. The supervisor should not say "no" and close the subject.
7. Fear and worry slow up a worker's ability. Poor working environment can impair his physical and mental health. A good supervisor avoids forceful methods, threats and arguments to get a job done.
8. A forceful supervisor is able to train his employees individually and as a team, and is able to motivate them in the proper channels.
9. A mature supervisor is able to properly evaluate his subordinates and to keep them happy and satisfied.
10. A sensitive supervisor will never patronize his subordinates.
11. A worthy supervisor will respect his employees' confidences.
12. Definite and clear-cut responsibilities should be assigned to each executive.
13. Responsibility should always be coupled with corresponding authority.
14. No change should be made in the scope or responsibilities of a position without a definite understanding to that effect on the part of all persons concerned.
15. No executive or employee, occupying a single position in the organization, should be subject to definite orders from more than one source.
16. Orders should never be given to subordinates over the head of a responsible executive. Rather than do this, the officer in question should be supplanted.
17. Criticisms of subordinates should, whoever possible, be made privately, and in no case should a subordinate be criticized in the presence of executives or employees of equal or lower rank.
18. No dispute or difference between executives or employees as to authority or responsibilities should be considered too trivial for prompt and careful adjudication.
19. Promotions, wage changes, and disciplinary action should always be approved by the executive immediately superior to the one directly responsible.
20. No executive or employee should ever be required, or expected, to be at the same time an assistant to, and critic of, another.
21. Any executive whose work is subject to regular inspection should, whever practicable, be given the assistance and facilities necessary to enable him to maintain an independent check of the quality of his work.

VIII. MINI-TEXT IN SUPERVISION, ADMINISTRATION, MANAGEMENT, AND ORGANIZATION

A. BRIEF HIGHLIGHTS

Listed concisely and sequentially are major headings and important data in the field for quick recall and review.

1. *LEVELS OF MANAGEMENT*

Any organization of some size has several levels of management. In terms of a ladder the levels are:

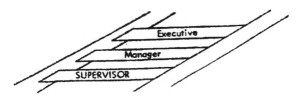

The first level is very important because it is the beginning point of management leadership.

2. WHAT THE SUPERVISOR MUST LEARN

A supervisor must learn to:
  (1) Deal with people and their differences
  (2) Get the job done through people
  (3) Recognize the problems when they exist
  (4) Overcome obstacles to good performance
  (5) Evaluate the performance of people
  (6) Check his own performance in terms of accomplishment

3. A DEFINITION OF SUPERVISOR

The term supervisor means any individual having authority, in the interests of the employer, to hire, transfer, suspend, lay-off, recall, promote, discharge, assign, reward, or discipline other employees or responsibility to direct them, or to adjust their grievances, or effectively to recommend such action, if, in connection with the foregoing, exercise of such authority is not of a merely routine or clerical nature but requires the use of independent judgment.

4. ELEMENTS OF THE TEAM CONCEPT

What is involved in teamwork? The component parts are:
  (1) Members   (3) Goals   (5) Cooperation
  (2) A leader   (4) Plans   (6) Spirit

5. PRINCIPLES OF ORGANIZATION

  (1) A team member must know what his job is.
  (2) Be sure that the nature and scope of a job are understood.
  (3) Authority and responsibility should be carefully spelled out.
  (4) A supervisor should be permitted to make the maximum number of decisions affecting his employees.
  (5) Employees should report to only one supervisor.
  (6) A supervisor should direct only as many employees as he can handle effectively.
  (7) An organization plan should be flexible.
  (8) Inspection and performance of work should be separate.
  (9) Organizational problems should receive immediate attention.
  (10) Assign work in line with ability and experience.

6. THE FOUR IMPORTANT PARTS OF EVERY JOB

  (1) Inherent in every job is the *accountability* for results.
  (2) A second set of factors in every job is *responsibilities.*
  (3) Along with duties and responsibilities one must have the *authority* to act within certain limits without obtaining permission to proceed.
  (4) No job exists in a vacuum. The supervisor is surrounded by key *relationships.*

7. PRINCIPLES OF DELEGATION

Where work is delegated for the first time, the supervisor should think in terms of these questions:
  (1) Who is best qualified to do this?
  (2) Can an employee improve his abilities by doing this?
  (3) How long should an employee spend on this?
  (4) Are there any special problems for which he will need guidance?
  (5) How broad a delegation can I make?

8. PRINCIPLES OF EFFECTIVE COMMUNICATIONS
(1) Determine the media
(2) To whom directed?
(3) Identification and source authority
(4) Is communication understood?

9. PRINCIPLES OF WORK IMPROVEMENT
(1) Most people usually do only the work which is assigned to them
(2) Workers are likely to fit assigned work into the time available to perform it
(3) A good workload usually stimulates output
(4) People usually do their best work when they know that results will be reviewed or inspected
(5) Employees usually feel that someone else is responsible for conditions of work, workplace layout, job methods, type of tools/equipment, and other such factors
(6) Employees are usually defensive about their job security
(7) Employees have natural resistance to change
(8) Employees can support or destroy a supervisor
(9) A supervisor usually earns the respect of his people through his personal example of diligence and efficiency

10. AREAS OF JOB IMPROVEMENT
The areas of job improvement are quite numerous, but the most common ones which a supervisor can identify and utilize are:

(1) Departmental layout
(2) Flow of work
(3) Workplace layout
(4) Utilization of manpower
(5) Work methods
(6) Materials handling
(7) Utilization
(8) Motion economy

11. SEVEN KEY POINTS IN MAKING IMPROVEMENTS
(1) Select the job to be improved
(2) Study how it is being done now
(3) Question the present method
(4) Determine actions to be taken
(5) Chart proposed method
(6) Get approval and apply
(7) Solicit worker participation

12. CORRECTIVE TECHNIQUES OF JOB IMPROVEMENT

Specific Problems	General Improvement	Corrective Techniques
(1) Size of workload	(1) Departmental layout	(1) Study with scale model
(2) Inability to meet schedules	(2) Flow of work	(2) Flow chart study
(3) Strain and fatigue	(3) Work plan layout	(3) Motion analysis
(4) Improper use of men and skills	(4) Utilization of manpower	(4) Comparison of units produced to standard allowance
(5) Waste, poor quality, unsafe conditions	(5) Work methods	(5) Methods analysis
(6) Bottleneck conditions that hinder output	(6) Materials handling	(6) Flow chart & equipment study
(7) Poor utilization of equipment and machine	(7) Utilization of equipment	(7) Down time vs. running time
(8) Efficiency and productivity of labor	(8) Motion economy	(8) Motion analysis

13. A *PLANNING CHECKLIST*

(1) Objectives   (6) Resources   (11) Safety
(2) Controls   (7) Manpower   (12) Money
(3) Delegations   (8) Equipment   (13) Work
(4) Communications   (9) Supplies and materials   (14) Timing of improvements
(5) Resources   (10) Utilization of time

14. *FIVE CHARACTERISTICS OF GOOD DIRECTIONS*

In order to get results, directions must be:

(1) Possible of accomplishment   (3) Related to mission   (5) Unmistakably clear
(2) Agreeable with worker interests   (4) Planned and complete

15. *TYPES OF DIRECTIONS*

(1) Demands or direct orders   (3) Suggestion or implication
(2) Requests   (4) Volunteering

16. *CONTROLS*

A typical listing of the overall areas in which the supervisor should establish controls might be:

(1) Manpower   (3) Quality of work   (5) Time   (7) Money
(2) Materials   (4) Quantity of work   (6) Space   (8) Methods

17. *ORIENTING THE NEW EMPLOYEE*

(1) Prepare for him   (3) Orientation for the job
(2) Welcome the new employee   (4) Follow-up

18. *CHECKLIST FOR ORIENTING NEW EMPLOYEES*   Yes   No

(1) Do your appreciate the feelings of new employees when they first report for work? ___ ___
(2) Are you aware of the fact that the new employee must make a big adjustment to his job? ___ ___
(3) Have you given him good reasons for liking the job and the organization? ___ ___
(4) Have you prepared for his first day on the job?
(5) Did you welcome him cordially and make him feel needed?
(6) Did you establish rapport with him so that he feels free to talk and discuss matters with you? ___ ___
(7) Did you explain his job to him and his relationship to you? ___ ___
(8) Does he know that his work will be evaluated periodically on a basis that is fair and objective? ___ ___
(9) Did you introduce him to his fellow workers in such a way that they are likely to accept him? ___ ___
(10) Does he know what employee benefits he will receive?
(11) Does he understand the importance of being on the job and what to do if he must leave his duty station? ___ ___
(12) Has he been impressed with the importance of accident prevention and safe practice? ___ ___
(13) Does he generally know his way around the department? ___ ___
(14) Is he under the guidance of a sponsor who will teach the right ways of doing things? ___ ___
(15) Do you plan to follow-up so that he will continue to adjust successfully to his job? ___ ___

19. *PRINCIPLES OF LEARNING*
      (1) Motivation   (2) Demonstration or explanation   (3) Practice

20. *CAUSES OF POOR PERFORMANCE*
    (1) Improper training for job
    (2) Wrong tools
    (3) Inadequate directions
    (4) Lack of supervisory follow-up
    (5) Poor communications
    (6) Lack of standards of performance
    (7) Wrong work habits
    (8) Low morale
    (9) Other

21. *FOUR MAJOR STEPS IN ON-THE-JOB INSTRUCTION*
    (1) Prepare the worker
    (2) Present the operation
    (3) Tryout performance
    (4) Follow-up

22. *EMPLOYEES WANT FIVE THINGS*
    (1) Security (2) Opportunity (3) Recognition (4) Inclusion (5) Expression

23. *SOME DON'TS IN REGARD TO PRAISE*
    (1) Don't praise a person for something he hasn't done
    (2) Don't praise a person unless you can be sincere
    (3) Don't be sparing in praise just because your superior withholds it from you
    (4) Don't let too much time elapse between good performance and recognition of it

24. *HOW TO GAIN YOUR WORKERS' CONFIDENCE*
Methods of developing confidence include such things as:
    (1) Knowing the interests, habits, hobbies of employees
    (2) Admitting your own inadequacies
    (3) Sharing and telling of confidence in others
    (4) Supporting people when they are in trouble
    (5) Delegating matters that can be well handled
    (6) Being frank and straightforward about problems and working conditions
    (7) Encouraging others to bring their problems to you
    (8) Taking action on problems which impede worker progress

25. *SOURCES OF EMPLOYEE PROBLEMS*
On-the-job causes might be such things as:
    (1) A feeling that favoritism is exercised in assignments
    (2) Assignment of overtime
    (3) An undue amount of supervision
    (4) Changing methods or systems
    (5) Stealing of ideas or trade secrets
    (6) Lack of interest in job
    (7) Threat of reduction in force
    (8) Ignorance or lack of communications
    (9) Poor equipment
    (10) Lack of knowing how supervisor feels toward employee
    (11) Shift assignments

Off-the-job problems might have to do with:
    (1) Health   (2) Finances   (3) Housing   (4) Family

26. *THE SUPERVISOR'S KEY TO DISCIPLINE*
There are several key points about discipline which the supervisor should keep in mind:
(1) Job discipline is one of the disciplines of life and is directed by the supervisor.
(2) It is more important to correct an employee fault than to fix blame for it.
(3) Employee performance is affected by problems both on the job and off.
(4) Sudden or abrupt changes in behavior can be indications of important employee problems.
(5) Problems should be dealt with as soon as possible after they are identified.
(6) The attitude of the supervisor may have more to do with solving problems than the techniques of problem solving.
(7) Correction of employee behavior should be resorted to only after the supervisor is sure that training or counseling will not be helpful.
(8) Be sure to document your disciplinary actions.
(9) Make sure that you are disciplining on the basis of facts rather than personal feelings.
(10) Take each disciplinary step in order, being careful not to make snap judgments, or decisions based on impatience.

27. *FIVE IMPORTANT PROCESSES OF MANAGEMENT*
(1) Planning
(2) Organizing
(3) Scheduling
(4) Controlling
(5) Motivating

28. *WHEN THE SUPERVISOR FAILS TO PLAN*
(1) Supervisor creates impression of not knowing his job
(2) May lead to excessive overtime
(3) Job runs itself -- supervisor lacks control
(4) Deadlines and appointments missed
(5) Parts of the work go undone
(6) Work interrupted by emergencies
(7) Sets a bad example
(8) Uneven workload creates peaks and valleys
(9) Too much time on minor details at expense of more important tasks

29. *FOURTEEN GENERAL PRINCIPLES OF MANAGEMENT*
(1) Division of work
(2) Authority and responsibility
(3) Discipline
(4) Unity of command
(5) Unity of direction
(6) Subordination of individual interest to general interest
(7) Remuneration of personnel
(8) Centralization
(9) Scalar chain
(10) Order
(11) Equity
(12) Stability of tenure of personnel
(13) Initiative
(14) Esprit de corps

30. *CHANGE*
Bringing about change is perhaps attempted more often, and yet less well understood, than anything else the supervisor does. How do people generally react to change? (People tend to resist change that is imposed upon them by other individuals or circumstances.

Change is characteristic of every situation. It is a part of every real endeavor where the efforts of people are concerned.

A. Why do people resist change?
    People may resist change because of:
        (1) Fear of the unknown
        (2) Implied criticism
        (3) Unpleasant experiences in the past
        (4) Fear of loss of status
        (5) Threat to the ego
        (6) Fear of loss of economic stability

B. How can we best overcome the resistance to change?
    In initiating change, take these steps:
        (1) Get ready to sell
        (2) Identify sources of help
        (3) Anticipate objections
        (4) Sell benefits
        (5) Listen in depth
        (6) Follow up

B. BRIEF TOPICAL SUMMARIES

I. WHO/WHAT IS THE SUPERVISOR?
1. The supervisor is often called the "highest level employee and the lowest level manager."
2. A supervisor is a member of both management and the work group. He acts as a bridge between the two.
3. Most problems in supervision are in the area of human relations, or people problems.
4. Employees expect: Respect, opportunity to learn and to advance, and a sense of belonging, and so forth.
5. Supervisors are responsible for directing people and organizing work. Planning is of paramount importance.
6. A position description is a set of duties and responsibilities inherent to a given position.
7. It is important to keep the position description up-to-date and to provide each employee with his own copy.

II. THE SOCIOLOGY OF WORK
1. People are alike in many ways; however, each individual is unique.
2. The supervisor is challenged in getting to know employee differences. Acquiring skills in evaluating individuals is an asset.
3. Maintaining meaningful working relationships in the organization is of great importance.
4. The supervisor has an obligation to help individuals to develop to their fullest potential.
5. Job rotation on a planned basis helps to build versatility and to maintain interest and enthusiasm in work groups.
6. Cross training (job rotation) provides backup skills.
7. The supervisor can help reduce tension by maintaining a sense of humor, providing guidance to employees, and by making reasonable and timely decisions. Employees respond favorably to working under reasonably predictable circumstances.
8. Change is characteristic of all managerial behavior. The supervisor must adjust to changes in procedures, new methods, technological changes, and to a number of new and sometimes challenging situations.
9. To overcome the natural tendency for people to resist change, the supervisor should become more skillful in initiating change.

III. PRINCIPLES AND PRACTICES OF SUPERVISION

1. Employees should be required to answer to only one superior.
2. A supervisor can effectively direct only a limited number of employees, depending upon the complexity, variety, and proximity of the jobs involved.
3. The organizational chart presents the organization in graphic form. It reflects lines of authority and responsibility as well as interrelationships of units within the organization.
4. Distribution of work can be improved through an analysis using the "Work Distribution Chart."
5. The "Work Distribution Chart" reflects the division of work within a unit in understandable form.
6. When related tasks are given to an employee, he has a better chance of increasing his skills through training.
7. The individual who is given the responsibility for tasks must also be given the appropriate authority to insure adequate results.
8. The supervisor should delegate repetitive, routine work. Preparation of recurring reports, maintaining leave and attendance records are some examples.
9. Good discipline is essential to good task performance. Discipline is reflected in the actions of employees on the job in the absence of supervision.
10. Disciplinary action may have to be taken when the positive aspects of discipline have failed. Reprimand, warning, and suspension are examples of disciplinary action.
11. If a situation calls for a reprimand, be sure it is deserved and remember it is to be done in private.

IV. DYNAMIC LEADERSHIP

1. A style is a personal method or manner of exerting influence.
2. Authoritarian leaders often see themselves as the source of power and authority.
3. The democratic leader often perceives the group as the source of authority and power.
4. Supervisors tend to do better when using the pattern of leadership that is most natural for them.
5. Social scientists suggest that the effective supervisor use the leadership style that best fits the problem or circumstances involved.
6. All four styles -- telling, selling, consulting, joining -- have their place. Using one does not preclude using the other at another time.
7. The theory X point of view assumes that the average person dislikes work, will avoid it whenever possible, and must be coerced to achieve organizational objectives.
8. The theory Y point of view assumes that the average person considers work to be as natural as play, and, when the individual is committed, he requires little supervision or direction to accomplish desired objectives.
9. The leader's basic assumptions concerning human behavior and human nature affect his actions, decisions, and other managerial practices.
10. Dissatisfaction among employees is often present, but difficult to isolate. The supervisor should seek to weaken dissatisfaction by keeping promises, being sincere and considerate, keeping employees informed, and so forth.
11. Constructive suggestions should be encouraged during the natural progress of the work.

V. PROCESSES FOR SOLVING PROBLEMS

1. People find their daily tasks more meaningful and satisfying when they can improve them.
2. The causes of problems, or the key factors, are often hidden in the background. Ability to solve problems often involves the ability to isolate them from their backgrounds. There is some substance to the cliché that some persons "can't see the forest for the trees."
3. New procedures are often developed from old ones. Problems should be broken down into manageable parts. New ideas can be adapted from old ones.

4. People think differently in problem-solving situations. Using a logical, patterned approach is often useful. One approach found to be useful includes these steps:

    (a) Define the problem   (d) Weigh and decide
    (b) Establish objectives   (e) Take action
    (c) Get the facts   (f) Evaluate action

VI. TRAINING FOR RESULTS

1. Participants respond best when they feel training is important to them.
2. The supervisor has responsibility for the training and development of those who report to him.
3. When training is delegated to others, great care must be exercised to insure the trainer has knowledge, aptitude, and interest for his work as a trainer.
4. Training (learning) of some type goes on continually. The most successful supervisor makes certain the learning contributes in a productive manner to operational goals.
5. New employees are particularly susceptible to training. Older employees facing new job situations require specific training, as well as having need for development and growth opportunities.
6. Training needs require continuous monitoring.
7. The training officer of an agency is a professional with a responsibility to assist supervisors in solving training problems.
8. Many of the self-development steps important to the supervisor's own growth are equally important to the development of peers and subordinates. Knowledge of these is important when the supervisor consults with others on development and growth opportunities.

VII. HEALTH, SAFETY, AND ACCIDENT PREVENTION

1. Management-minded supervisors take appropriate measures to assist employees in maintaining health and in assuring safe practices in the work environment.
2. Effective safety training and practices help to avoid injury and accidents.
3. Safety should be a management goal. All infractions of safety which are observed should be corrected without exception.
4. Employees' safety attitude, training and instruction, provision of safe tools and equipment, supervision, and leadership are considered highly important factors which contribute to safety and which can be influenced directly by supervisors.
5. When accidents do occur they should be investigated promptly for very important reasons, including the fact that information which is gained can be used to prevent accidents in the future.

VIII. EQUAL EMPLOYMENT OPPORTUNITY

1. The supervisor should endeavor to treat all employees fairly, without regard to religion, race, sex, or national origin.
2. Groups tend to reflect the attitude of the leader. Prejudice can be detected even in very subtle form. Supervisors must strive to create a feeling of mutual respect and confidence in every employee.
3. Complete utilization of all human resources is a national goal. Equitable consideration should be accorded women in the work force, minority-group members, the physically and mentally handicapped, and the older employee. The important question is: "Who can do the job?"
4. Training opportunities, recognition for performance, overtime assignments, promotional opportunities, and all other personnel actions are to be handled on an equitable basis.

IX. IMPROVING COMMUNICATIONS

1. Communications is achieving understanding between the sender and the receiver of a message. It also means sharing information -- the creation of understanding.
2. Communication is basic to all human activity. Words are means of conveying meanings; however, real meanings are in people.
3. There are very practical differences in the effectiveness of one-way, impersonal, and two-way communications. Words spoken face-to-face are better understood. Telephone conversations are effective, but lack the rapport of person-to-person exchanges. The whole person communicates.
4. Cooperation and communication in an organization go hand in hand. When there is a mutual respect between people, spelling out rules and procedures for communicating is unnecessary.
5. There are several barriers to effective communications. These include failure to listen with respect and understanding, lack of skill in feedback, and misinterpreting the meanings of words used by the speaker. It is also common practice to listen to what we want to hear, and tune out things we do not want to hear.
6. Communication is management's chief problem. The supervisor should accept the challenge to communicate more effectively and to improve interagency and intra-agency communications.
7. The supervisor may often plan for and conduct meetings. The planning phase is critical and may determine the success or the failure of a meeting.
8. Speaking before groups usually requires extra effort. Stage fright may never disappear completely, but it can be controlled.

X. SELF-DEVELOPMENT

1. Every employee is responsible for his own self-development.
2. Toastmaster and toastmistress clubs offer opportunities to improve skills in oral communications.
3. Planning for one's own self-development is of vital importance. Supervisors know their own strengths and limitations better than anyone else.
4. Many opportunities are open to aid the supervisor in his developmental efforts, including job assignments; training opportunities, both governmental and non-governmental -- to include universities and professional conferences and seminars.
5. Programmed instruction offers a means of studying at one's own rate.
6. Where difficulties may arise from a supervisor's being away from his work for training, he may participate in televised home study or correspondence courses to meet his self-develop- ment needs.

XI. TEACHING AND TRAINING

A. The Teaching Process

Teaching is encouraging and guiding the learning activities of students toward established goals. In most cases this process consists in five steps: preparation, presentation, summarization, evaluation, and application.

1. Preparation

Preparation is twofold in nature; that of the supervisor and the employee.
Preparation by the supervisor is absolutely essential to success. He must know what, when, where, how, and whom he will teach. Some of the factors that should be considered are:

(1) The objectives
(2) The materials needed
(3) The methods to be used
(4) Employee participation
(5) Employee interest
(6) Training aids
(7) Evaluation
(8) Summarization

Employee preparation consists in preparing the employee to receive the material. Probably the most important single factor in the preparation of the employee is arousing and maintaining his interest. He must know the objectives of the training, why he is there, how the material can be used, and its importance to him.

2. Presentation
In presentation, have a carefully designed plan and follow it.
The plan should be accurate and complete, yet flexible enough to meet situations as they arise. The method of presentation will be determined by the particular situation and objectives.

3. Summary
A summary should be made at the end of every training unit and program. In addition, there may be internal summaries depending on the nature of the material being taught. The important thing is that the trainee must always be able to understand how each part of the new material relates to the whole.

4. Application
The supervisor must arrange work so the employee will be given a chance to apply new knowledge or skills while the material is still clear in his mind and interest is high. The trainee does not really know whether he has learned the material until he has been given a chance to apply it. If the material is not applied, it loses most of its value.

5. Evaluation

The purpose of all training is to promote learning. To determine whether the training has been a success or failure, the supervisor must evaluate this learning.

In the broadest sense evaluation includes all the devices, methods, skills, and techniques used by the supervisor to keep him self and the employees informed as to their progress toward the objectives they are pursuing. The extent to which the employee has mastered the knowledge, skills, and abilities, or changed his attitudes, as determined by the program objectives, is the extent to which instruction has succeeded or failed.

Evaluation should not be confined to the end of the lesson, day, or program but should be used continuously. We shall note later the way this relates to the rest of the teaching process.

B. Teaching Methods

A teaching method is a pattern of identifiable student and instructor activity used in presenting training material.

All supervisors are faced with the problem of deciding which method should be used at a given time.

As with all methods, there are certain advantages and disadvantages to each method.

1. Lecture
The lecture is direct oral presentation of material by the supervisor. The present trend is to place less emphasis on the trainer's activity and more on that of the trainee.

2. Discussion
Teaching by discussion or conference involves using questions and other techniques to arouse interest and focus attention upon certain areas, and by doing so creating a learning situation. This can be one of the most valuable methods because it gives the employees 'an opportunity to express their ideas and pool their knowledge.

3. Demonstration

The demonstration is used to teach how something works or how to do something. It can be used to show a principle or what the results of a series of actions will be. A well-staged demonstration is particularly effective because it shows proper methods of performance in a realistic manner.

4. Performance

Performance is one of the most fundamental of all learning techniques or teaching methods. The trainee may be able to tell how a specific operation should be performed but he cannot be sure he knows how to perform the operation until he has done so.

5. Which Method to Use

Moreover, there are other methods and techniques of teaching. It is difficult to use any method without other methods entering into it. In any learning situation a combination of methods is usually more effective than anyone method alone.

Finally, evaluation must be integrated into the other aspects of the teaching-learning process.

It must be used in the motivation of the trainees; it must be used to assist in developing understanding during the training; and it must be related to employee application of the results of training.

This is distinctly the role of the supervisor.

———